LOST INHERITANCE

LOST INHERITANCE

BARUCH

Copyright © 2021 by Baruch.

ISBN:	eBook	978-0-6453703-1-7
	Softcover	978-0-6453703-0-0

All rights reserved. No part of this book may be reproduced or transmitted in any form or by any means, electronic or mechanical, including photocopying, recording, or by any information storage and retrieval system, without permission in writing from the copyright owner.

Rev. date: 01/12/2021

CONTENTS

PROLOGUE.................... vii

Chapter 1	My Forebears...	1
Chapter 2	The Colonization of Rhodesia	5
Chapter 3	The Spoil of War	11
Chapter 4	The Winds of Change	16
Chapter 5	Lost Inheritance	22
Chapter 6	Life at Springvale	26
Chapter 7	The Accident at Springvale	32
Chapter 8	Servitude	37
Chapter 9	Life in Shabani	53
Chapter 10	Boarding School	58
Chapter 11	The Rise of African Nationalism and Bush War	70
Chapter 12	National Service	75
Chapter 13	My Employment and Marriage	81
Chapter 14	Ava's Marriage	92
Chapter 15	Territorial Service	97
Chapter 16	The Extended Family	101
Chapter 17	My Business Ventures	104
Chapter 18	Zimbabwe Political and Economic Decline	109
Chapter 19	My Debilitating Illness	121

Epilogue..127

PROLOGUE

MZILIKAZI, (PRONOUNCED MZILI-GAZI meaning "the trail of blood"), was a Southern African king who founded the Khumalo kingdom of Matabeleland. His kingdom was later overrun by the British South Africa Company of Cecil John Rhodes, to become Rhodesia and, later, Zimbabwe. He was the son of *uMatshobana* and was born in 1790 near *Mkuze*, Zululand (now part of South Africa). He died at the age of 78 years at Ingama in Matabeleland near *koBulawayo* in 1868. He was, according to popular belief, the greatest military commander to come out of Sub-Saharan Africa after the great Zulu King, Tshaka.

Mzilikazi was about three years younger than *Tshaka*. As a leading general in Tshaka's army, he became widely respected within the kingdom for his daring raids and his ruthlessness. Even king Tshaka had a high regard for him.

Sometime in 1823, *Tshaka* sent *Mzilikazi* on a punitive raid against one chief. He was successful. As he was returning, he sent word to the king asking to be allowed to keep some of the spoils from the raid. The king declined and, sensing the wrath of the king, *Mzilikazi* and the *Khumalo* clan fled to a spot near the modern town of Bethal, some 150 kilometres from Johannesburg. They named their new home *ekuPhumuleni* or "place of rest" where they remained for a while because the rains were good and the soils rich. This brought prosperity for the exiles.

As their herds grew, the new king worried that *Tshaka* would hear of their good fortune and grow jealous and so, he moved his people to where Pretoria now stands, and then Brits, and finally to a site on the Groot Marico River near Botswana.

Afraid to face ritual execution, *Mzilikazi* continued to flee northward with his tribe. Amongst those that accompanied Mzilikazi was Chief *Mhabahaba Mkwananzi* of the *Abezansi* clan and leader of the *Intuta* Regiment.

Mzilikazi would eventually take his tribe, the Khumalo, on an 800 kilometres (500 miles) journey from the Zulu kingdom to what is now called Zimbabwe.

First, he travelled towards Mozambique. In 1826, he moved west to avoid continued attacks from his enemies. Whilst in the Transvaal, he conquered and also absorbed many members of other groups and established a military dictatorship. He exhibited significant statesmanship and ability to weld his own people and the many tribes he conquered, into a large, formidable and diverse but centralized kingdom.

For the next decade, the entire northern region of South Africa was dominated by Mzilikazi and his warriors. He destroyed local kingdoms and pushed others, like the Shangaans, Venda, Pedi and Tswana off the best land. This period, which was characterized by devastation and murder at a grand scale, was designed to instill fear and keep all surrounding kingdoms at a distance. He removed all opposition. He also remodeled the territory to suit the new Ndebele order. This period was known as "*Mfecane*" or "The Crushing".

The death toll has never been accurately determined. Because of the region's extensive depopulation, the *Voortrekkers* were able to occupy and take ownership of the Highveld without any opposition in the 1830s. They were named *amaNdebele* by their rivals, which means "the people of tall shields".

Historical records reveal that, during its ascendency, the Roman Empire achieved greatness because, on conquering another nation or country, it would invariably incorporate those that had surrendered into its ranks to create an even greater force. Likewise, Mzilikazi adopted this strategy to build and grow his force. It was in using this method that the Matabele built their numbers.

In this fashion a nation was born. As each tribe was conquered, the Ndebele incorporated those who had surrendered, to create an even greater force.

As a general rule and, as a matter of practice, men and women of working age who would not willingly submit to the new order were taken as slaves. As difficult as it may be to understand in this modern era, this practice is in line with that employed by the great empires, such as the Mongol Empire or Incas of South America and, even the Yuan Dynasty. In this respect, and without any doubt, *Tshaka* was the biggest slave owner in Southern Africa and Mzilikazi came, indisputably, a close second.

In situations where villages were pillaged and plundered, those that were left would starve. Their only option was to align themselves with the winning tribe or become their slaves. Those taken as slaves were later released and assimilated into the new society and, eventually becoming full citizens.

The Zulu language benefitted immensely from Mfecane as the language of those conquered was absorbed into the isiNdebele language, adding a greater number of words to the original Zulu language, along with variations of pitch and tone. Although now, somewhat different from the Zulu language, a Zulu person will spot a Matabele as soon as the person speaks.

By 1830, the area ruled by Mzilikazi had spread. It covered modern- day Gauteng and much of the Orange Free State, Mpumalanga, Limpopo and part of the North West.

Boys were tasked to herd livestock from the age of seven or eight. They spent their leisure time talking of the day they would be old enough to join the army. By the age of 12, they were physically strong and able to drive cattle for 10 hours and walk barefoot over stones, without cutting their feet.

The Matabele could count but had no starting point. Years were numbered in relation to various events. For example, someone was born two seasons before the invasion of the locusts or at the time when the lightning killed 20 goats on a hilltop. As a result, few could be sure of how old they were.

Zulu traditions were maintained. Young men were all conscripted into regiments on attaining a certain age. However, to determine age and maturity, each teenager would stand naked in front of the unit commander and, if the recruit looked as if he was close to manhood, he was allowed to proceed. If, on the other hand, he appeared to be still in the early stages of puberty, he had to wait another year. All young men in regiments were forbidden to marry without the permission of the king.

Women also had roles according to their age and there was a strict code of respect and behaviour. Planting, cooking, harvesting, collecting water, wood and wild fruit and carrying out household chores were all important duties as well as the most treasured roll of raising children.

Mzilikazi was expected to sit in judgment over all disputes between his subjects. However, before any matters could be referred to him, they would go before the induna or chief and, if nothing was resolved, the king held court and his word was final.

It was at this time that the first white missionaries and explorers began to enter the region. They were all welcome, provided they sort permission from the king to pass through the land. They were also welcome to call upon the king who reserved his right to grant or refuse them audience.

Robert Moffat, who had set up a mission at Kuruman in the Northern Cape, and his son-in-law, David Livingstone, were among his regular visitors. There were, also, some French and American missionaries who had asked for permission to settle in the area under his protection. Nor were they only kept safe but came to be looked upon as friends.

Dr. Moffat, who spoke Zulu fluently, was very liked by Mzilikazi to the extent that Mzilikazi named his first born son "Nkulumana" as an honour to Moffat's mission at Kuruman (note here the Ndebele corruption of the word Kuruman. There is no letter "R" in the Ndebele language or alphabet). The two men became so close that the king referred to him as, "my special guest" The two men would sit up all night talking politics, while the missionary tried in vain to convert his host to the Church.

In the Ndebele calendar of events, there were feast days and celebrations; the first rains, first fruits on the trees, birth of the impala antelope in the wild (around December), flooding of the rivers, and harvest of crops. At each of these events women would sing and warriors would dance. The nation came together in unity. The nation was reaffirming itself before the ancestral spirits and, to every member of the tribe, as a people united by the language, culture, tradition and loyalty to the king and to each other. The Matabele nation was here to stay.

There was, however, change in the horizon. The great king Tshaka had been assassinated and replaced by king Dingaan. King Dingaan had heard exaggerated reports about the wealth of Mzilikazi. He had been told that Mzilikazi's cattle were so numerous that they stretched over plains into mountains and on through neighbouring valleys, almost without end. On the other hand, a series of droughts had cut the Zulu herd, and Dingaan had decided to send his armies to raid the Matabele.

Meanwhile, almost a thousand kilometres away in the Eastern Cape, the new British rulers were sailing their ships, laden with farmers, tradesman and their families who, it was hoped, would develop the area around Port Elizabeth and East London.

On the other hand, the Dutch, who had been in the Cape since 1652, were not happy with the British influx. Large numbers packed their wagons and, in 1834, headed north. This became known as the Great Trek.

It was not until 1835 that these pioneers, forefathers of today's Afrikaners, arrived near the Vaal River. They crossed the river and established themselves less than 100 kilometres from the Matabele. They refused to seek permission from the king, unlike earlier travelers. It was evident that war was inevitable.

In 1836, more Voortrekkers began to arrive in the Transvaal. In August 1836, a Matabele patrol killed an Afrikaans hunting party. The Voortrekkers retaliated. Mzilikazi sent his army in response.

War between the Voortrekkers began in earnest on 16 October at the battle of Vegkop in Northern Free State. The Voortrekkers placed 50 wagons in a circle. They were able to hold off more than 4 000 warriors with their guns. The Matabele withdrew with most of their cattle and nearly 50 000 sheep.

Not long after this encounter, Dingaan's army made a surprise raid on the Matabele. While Mzilikazi's forces were regrouping, Voortrekkers attacked. The Ndebeles responded by burning their settlements and pushing north across the Limpopo.

Over the next two years, the Ndebele suffered heavy losses. This became too much for Mzilikazi and he decided to cross the Limpopo and out of the Transvaal altogether. Further attacks were made against his armies which made him to move west to present-day Botswana. Later, he moved north towards what is now Zambia where he couldn't settle due to the prevalence of tsetse fly. He therefore travelled southeastwards to what became known as Matabeleland. He settled there in 1840.

Whilst moving north, Mzilikazi split his army into two divisions. This was a tactic used by him when he feared that an enemy may be following. In this instance, however, the two divisions became separated. One was led by the king and the other by Gundwane "Mkalipi" Ndiweni and Mzilikazi's son, Nkulumana. Mzilikazi pushed in the land of the Tswana people. He then turned east about 80 kilometres from the Zambezi River. On the other hand, Gundwane, Nkulumana and the elderly, women and children marched across the Limpopo River and settled at the Matobo Hills.

There was no word from Mzilikazi for more than a year. In September 1839, as winter gave way to spring, custom demanded that the new settlement should celebrate *ncwala* or the ceremony of first fruits.

This could not be done without the presence of the king. Many believed that the king had died in the desert. After much consultation a decision was taken by a section of the chiefs or indunas to place Nkulumana on the throne.

Mzilikazi and his group were not far from Hwange National Park when word reached him that he had been replaced. After calling his followers together he marched south, finally reuniting with his other group or division early in 1840.

Nkulumana sent a party to meet his father. The king hearing that they really had thought him dead, forgave the treason until, that is, he asked what great sorrow and mourning had filled the land on news of his death.

He learned that the settlers had not held the usual ceremonies on the loss of a king. Their excuse had been that they were exhausted from their journey. Mzilikazi was livid and furious. He had Nkulumana and all the other sons and their advisors taken to a nearby hill and executed. Today, that mountain is known as iNtabazinduna or hill of chiefs.

So many, it seems, had died from the royal house that day. This incident gave rise to a fresh name to be given for the site they had chosen as their new home. It was aptly named, "the place of great killing" or koBulawayo.

Prominent amongst those that had advocated for the installation of Nkulumana as king was chief Mhabahaba. He was one of Mzilikazi's trusted lieutenants whose association with Mzilikazi went back to the time when they both served under king Tshaka. He repented and had asked for Mzilikazi's forgiveness. Mzilikazi recognized Mhabahaba's action in the matter as an error of judgment and pardoned him. Mhabahaba was banished to live in Mberengwa among the vaRemba tribe. He later established the Ngungumbane chieftainship.

After his arrival in Matabeleland Mzilikazi continued to rule as he had done in the Transvaal. His followers were organized into a military system with regimental kraals similar to those of Tshaka. These were strong enough to repel the Boer attacks of 1847 – 1851. With this formidable strategy he was able to persuade the government of the South African Republic to sign a treaty with him in 1852.

Even when he had established himself as king in Matabeleland, he was generally friendly to European travelers. He was however mindful of the danger they posed to his kingdom. In later years he refused some visitors any access to his realm.

Mzilikazi met with many Europeans among whom were Henry Hartley, the hunter and explorer, Robert Moffat, the missionary, David Hume, the explorer and doctor, William Cornwallis, ethnologist and zoologist and David Livingstone, missionary/explorer.

Mzilikazi made his capital 5 kilometres (3.1 mi) from iNtabazinduna and named it koBulawayo (place of slaughter). Mhabahaba Mkwananzi established his Intuta Village at eMalungwane near Fort Rixon where the Ngungumbane clan remained until 1929 when the chieftainship was relocated to Mberengwa.

Mzilikazi died in 1868. The *izinduna* offered the crown to Lobengula, one of Mzilikazi's sons from an inferior wife. This was disputed by several impis (regiments). The question of Lobengula's ascent to the throne was ultimately decided by a clash of arms. Lobengula and his *impis* crushed the rebels. Lobengula's bravery in the battle led to his unanimous selection as king.

Lobengula was crowned at Mhlanhlandlela which was one of the principal military towns. This was a spectacular event with the Ndebele nation assembled in a large semicircle and performing a war dance. They declared their willingness to fight and die for Lobengula. Many cattle were killed for the feast. The choicest meats were offered to Mlimo, the Ndebele spiritual leader as well as to Mzilikazi the deceased king. The attendees consumed a lot of millet beer.

Crowning of Lobengula was attended by about ten thousand warriors wearing full war costumes. The costumes consisted of a headdress and a short cape. The cape was made of black ostrich feathers. They also wore a kilt made of leopard or other skins. It was ornamented with the tails of white cattle.

Around their arms they wore similar tails. Around their ankles they wore rings of brass and other metals.

Their weapons consisted of one or more long spears for throwing. They also had a short stabbing spear or assegai. (This is also the principal weapon of the Zulu).

For defence, they carried large oval shields of ox-hide. These were black, white, red, or speckled according to the *impi* they belonged to.

The *Ndebele* were able to maintain their position due to tight discipline. Every able-bodied man in the tribe owed service to the army. The Ndebele army consisted of about 15,000 men in 40 regiments based around Lobengula's capital in the capital of Bulawayo.

CHAPTER 1

My Forebears

MY GREAT, GREAT paternal grandfather was William Holl the Elder thought to be a political radical.

He was born in 1771. He was an engraver having learned this trade under Benjamin Smith who practiced in the *Stipple Method*. He was particularly noted for his engraved portraits. These were very numerous with some being executed for *Lodge's Portraits* in 1821.

He was occupied in engraving Corbould's drawings of the antique marbles in the British Museum. Amongst some of his works, he engraved, "*The Boar that killed Adonis, brought before Venus*", after R. Westall.

He was modest and unobtrusive, and his works often appeared under the name of others. He held Liberal views in politics. During the *Spa Fields Riots* in December 1816, he exposed himself to great risk by hiding the ringleader, Watson.

He married Mary Ravenscroft, and they had four sons. The first born was named William (the Younger). All his sons were Engravers all taught by himself and all excellent engravers. His second son Benjamin, a Portrait and Figure engraver, born on the 11th March 1808, went to the U.S.A. His first published plate was the frontispiece *'William IV'* after A. Wivell (1832). He did some plates for H. Jordan's *National Portrait Gallery* (1830-34). He exhibited at the Society of British Artists, in 1828-29.

Charles, the third son, was also a Portrait and Figure Engraver. He worked in his brother William's Studio for thirty years. Among his many engravings were the "*The Agony*" after Dolci, "*Have Mercy upon me O God*" after *Guido*, "*Captive Israelites*" - after *Bendeman*, all published in the 'Book of Common Prayer, 1854'.

The youngest son Francis (1815-84), born on March 23rd, worked for twenty-five years on the Queen's pictures, as well as receiving commissions from the Queen to execute private of herself and other members of the Royal Family. He was elected a Member of the Royal Academy between 1856 and 1879. His son, Francis Montague (a.k.a. Frank Holl), was a brilliant artist, and exhibited ninety-one pictures in all, at the academy.

William Holl the Younger was born at Plaistow, Essex, in February 1807. He married Annie Faulkner on the 16th October 1852, in London. He was an eminent Landscape and Portrait Engraver to Royalty. "Rebekka" and "The Merrymakers" were among his many wonderful works. He learnt engraving from his father, whose stipple method he adopted for some time, though subsequently, he became a line engraver on steel. He engraved a series of twenty-one 'Portraits' for E. Lodge's 'Portraits', 2nd edition, 1835, which began in May, 1829, with "Thomas Cranmer", and ended in November 1835, with "Horatio, First Lord Walpole", after Vanloo.

Ten of his plates were issued in Wright's Gallery of engravings, 1844-46, and his Scripture engravings appeared in Fisher's Historic Illustrations of the Bible, (1840-43), which contained fourteen, after artists such as Rembrandt, B. West and J. Nortcote. His plate, of "Ruth and Naomi", after H. Lejeune, is remarkable, and nine engravings, done jointly with his brother Francis, of which the picture after Raphael, 'Unto us a child is born' is notable. He engraved "An English Merrymaking" after
W. P. Frith, R. A., and also 'The Village Pastor', 'The Cleaner, and his wife' and just before his death; he completed 'Rebekah' after F. Goodall for the Art Union of London. In the 1860's he was engaged in Portraits of the Royal Family, and in 1863, those of the Prince and Princess of Wales, after photographs by Mayall were issued, and were engraved in ten days, - the most creditable examples of art, combining great softness with richness of tone.

William Holl (the Younger) had nine children and their names were Florence, born 3 September 1853, William Ravenscroft, born 20 November 1854, Annie, born 17 February 1857, died 19/6/1858, Annie, born 26 January 1859, Kate, born 8 May 1861, Harry, born 27 March 1863, died 30 April 1866, Twins Ida & Ella, born 3 May 1865, and Harry Patrick, born

17 March 1868. Harry Patrick Holl was fondly called "Pat".

William Holl (the Younger) died in 1871. Annie, Pat's mother, after being widowed for some time, followed her son, Pat, to the Cape and there married a Captain Norris Newman, who was several years her junior, and who had previously been engaged to her oldest daughter, Florence. He turned to the mother, when he realized that she had inherited her entire husband's wealth. The couple then moved on to Bulawayo where they settled and lived during the First Matabele Rebellion.

As Pat was his father's only surviving son, he inherited his grandfather's Family Home, known as *'Ravenscroft'*, a lovely Old Manor House, with its own Family Burial Ground, which was in Kent and was named after his grandmother, Mary Ravenscroft. In addition, he inherited the beautiful huge leather-bound volumes of the Old and New Testaments of the Holl Family Bibles, which had many illustrations done by William Holl (the Younger) and Francis Holl. These were family treasures handed down from the oldest son to his son.

Harry Patrick Holl was born in St. Pancras, London on the 17 March 1868, and he died in Bulawayo, on the 8th September 1928 at the age of sixty years. He was the youngest of the family of nine children - two of whom had died in infancy.

Pat was a keen sportsman, a long-distance runner, a champion at putting-the-shot and pole-vaulting, and a top marathon cyclist.

He was not interested in a Professional Career. His one great love was an outdoor life, and his wish was to become a proficient mixed farmer. Nevertheless, he was a keen historian, and he had a fine library with many volumes of World History, and he inherited a selection of beautiful Engravings, done by his Forebears, including a volume of "100 *of the world's Most Famous Paintings"*, in colour.

As a young man of about twenty-two years of age, Pat came to South Africa from England, especially to learn farming. It was in the year 1890 that he cycled from Cape Town to the Eastern Cape and arrived in the Ladysmith area, where he met an elderly Boer Farmer, who was only too happy to take on an energetic and eager young man. He taught Pat everything he knew about mixed farming. Pat lived with the family, learning to converse with them; and there was mutual respect, understanding and enjoyment in all they did together.

The Boer Farmer had a lovely daughter, and inevitably, a gradual romance blossomed between the two-young people, over the next two or three years it was no surprise when Pat asked her parents for their daughter's hand in marriage which they fully approved. Life continued happily for them all. Alas, however, at about this time, the Anglo-Boer war escalated as history will confirm, and all Englishmen were called to arms. Unhappily, the situation between the Boer Nation and England became critical, and this state of affairs made life very difficult for Pat and his fiancée. He was in a dreadful dilemma. As an Englishman he could not be dishonourable to his country. He vowed that he would never fight against the Boer people. As a result of his decision, and after much heartbreak, and understanding on her family's part, the young couple's engagement was tearfully terminated.

CHAPTER 2

The Colonization of Rhodesia

THE IDEA TO colonize Africa was first mooted in 1885 when all the major power brokers of Europe met in Berlin to discuss how best to partition Africa between them with a minimum of conflict. They agreed amongst themselves that effective occupation and administration would represent an acceptable proof of annexation. A prerequisite for this would be some sort of friendship or an appeal for protection by whatever tribal leader or leadership that held sway over any particular area.

At various times in the past a commercial company would undertake the initial thrust of occupation. These companies would be embraced by very wide terms of reference defined by a Royal Charter awarded by the crown with a specific purpose of administering and exploiting a new territory. The British East India Company which administered and defended India provides a perfect example of how colonization worked.

During this period a man by the name of Cecil John Rhodes, a diamond magnate of considerable worth was the main British power broker. He was also an influential politician in the Cape Assembly. He was also one of the most determined and ambitious of the imperial lobby at the time. All the major European powers influential at the time – mainly Portugal and Germany, had expressed great interest in the unclaimed territory north of the Limpopo. Something of a mini- scramble took place to secure the strategic territory that would open the way north into the vast interior of Africa.

In order for Rhodes to secure a Royal Charter that would empower his British South Africa Company to move to occupy Mashonaland, it was necessary for him to secure a treaty from the powerful amaNdebele monarch, *Lobengula*. The *Rudd Concession* was the bedrock upon which white occupation of the territory that would later become Rhodesia was built.

The *amaNdebele* represented a powerful, widely influential monarch. The *amaNdebele* were very much like their distant cousins, the *Zulu*, unlike a majority of local or tribal groups from which treaties and concessions were extracted during the process of partitioning. Under either direct or indirect *amaNdebele* control, reinforced by a highly organized, disciplined and effective military structure, lay a large swath of territory.

To persuade *Lobengula* into signing what was in effect a limited mining concession within his territory required a great deal of coercion and no small amount of dishonesty. This was known as the *Rudd Concession* after the chief protagonist in the enterprise, Charles Dunell Rudd – upon which was framed an application to the British Government for granting of a Royal Charter; this application requiring some very skillful political lobbying in London in the spring of 1889 by Cecil Rhodes. The application was successful and was granted in October of that year.

With the granting of the *Rudd Concession* the stage was now set to colonize Mashonaland. The colonialists, under the leadership of Leander Starr Jameson, Frank Johnston and Frederick Courtney Selous gathered in the settlement of *Macloutsie* in present day Botswana. Accompanied by a corps of volunteers, they set out in May 1890 at the head of a large and well-defended column to carve a road through unmapped territory towards Mashonaland, an amaNdebele vassal territory and heartland of the Mashona language group. Included in this group, later known as the Pioneer Column, were 200 paramilitary volunteers known as the British South Africa Police.

At this time, *Lobengula* was still king and head of the powerful and irreconciled *amaNdebele* army. The leadership of the Ndebele people had rejected the terms of the Rudd Concession, as did *Lobengula* himself, once he came to realise what it meant in practical terms. They urged the king to wipe out the intruders with military force.

However, *Lobengula* recognised that such a radical course of action would not ultimately solve the problem of white interest in his territory but would, in reality, simply invite a more massive response from the increasingly white dominated south. He was well aware that a decade earlier, the *Zulu* nation, the model upon which the *amaNdebele* nation was founded, had been comprehensively defeated at the hands of the British in the Anglo/Zulu war of 1879.

Lobengula successfully restrained his belligerent army. The British South Africa Company Pioneer column successfully entered Mashonaland. They established the capital of the new colony and named it Fort Salisbury and renamed the territory, Rhodesia, in honour of Cecil John Rhodes. Also established at that time were two other administrative centres which were named Fort Charter and Fort Victoria.

The public subscription that had underwritten the British South Africa Company, and which largely financed the expedition, had been based on expectations that large reserves of gold lay beneath the soils of the newly colonized territory of Mashonaland which was effectively under the control of the British South Africa Company. Gold, however, was not found and many early pioneers left the territory in poverty, but new settlers arrived with fresh capital and enthusiasm. The settler community increased steadily, and the roots of a permanent white population began to spread throughout the colony.

Leander Starr Jameson was the first substantive administrator. Jameson had developed a personal rapport with *Lobengula* during the process of securing the *Rudd Concession* and ratifying its terms. The effects of the *Rudd Concession* were that Mashonaland became the territory of the British South Africa Company whilst Matabeleland remained under the direct control and occupation of the amaNdebele. It was the diplomatic relationship between Jameson and Lobengula that helped retain peace between the two territories.

Despite the peace and tranquility that existed between the parties, the difficulty in this situation lay in the fact that the amaNdebele continued to exist as a highly mobile and effective, and dangerous, military culture that adhered to rules of diplomacy and military deployment that were, at the very least, compatible with the current political reality of white Southern Africa. To the colonialists, it became obvious that the amaNdebele would have to be subdued. Bearing in mind the nature of the amaNdebele as a people, this would have to be in the form of a clash of arms.

The *amaNdebele* continued their efforts to retain their traditional control over the Mashona people. The *Mashona* people were now increasingly seeking and beginning to take for granted the protection of the white man. The colonialist seized this as an opportunity to go to war.

The *amaNdebele* continued their punitive raids into Mashonaland. This presented the British South Africa Company administration with a problem but also an ideal pretext for war. In the context of all this, Matabeleland was there for the taking. The question that remained was who would take the first step. Should the imperial forces (i.e. those armed and paid by the British Government) be involved in pacifying the amaNdebele, then Matabeleland would become, one way or another, a Crown territory – probably a protectorate but not an addition to the territory controlled by the British South Africa Company.

To enable Cecil John Rhodes and his British South Africa Company to claim Matabeleland as an addition to Rhodesia, it was essential that the military defeat of the amaNdebele be undertaken by company forces under company command. Unlike Matabeleland, Mashonaland did not have meaningful gold deposits. Consequently, it had not provided the anticipated profits. Considerable concern was evident among investors as the British South Africa Company shares were plummeting. Some new and potentially profitable addition to the company portfolio was urgently needed, and between Jameson and Rhodes, Matabeleland was identified as this.

War between the amaNdebele army and company volunteer units began in November 1893, beginning with a series of skirmishes which resulted in the rapid defeat of the amaNdebele impis and the occupation of the amaNdebele capital of koBulawayo. This resulted in Lobengula fleeing northwards with a large portion of his army still intact. In the aftermath of this the imperial army forces arrived on the scene which effectively allowed Rhodes to claim victory and annex Matabeleland as part of Rhodesia.

As Lobengula had not capitulated, nor terms of peace agreed upon, this meant that the amaNdebele nation was still at war. Notwithstanding, Matabeleland had been effectively occupied and the amaNdebele dispersed. Despite all this Lobengula was still at large and as such remained a rallying point. It was necessary to bring him in and thus began the iconic Shangani Patrol incident; details of which are not discussed in this book, which culminated in the death of Lobengula on 23rd January 1894.

Captain Charles Louis Norris Newman, Pat's stepfather, was the first war correspondent sent to Bulawayo in 1893 by Reuters to report on the Matabele uprising. Newman wrote a number of books. His book on "Matabeleland" was written in Bulawayo in 1894. Today it is part of the collection of Rhodesia in the Bulawayo public library.

Annie (Holl) Newman was the first lady resident in the lovely Bulawayo suburbs, where she had a large house built, and she remained in Bulawayo, during the harassing times of the "Laager" and Rebellion. She had come to Bulawayo as part of a large contingent of settlers following the defeat of the amaNdebele which had resulted in *Lobengula's* forced and hurried departure . . . She died on 5th April 1898, at her residence "Sherwood", and later, her body was exhumed, and Pat took her "remains" to be buried in England in the Family Graveyard, at "Ravenscroft", on the 11th July 1901.

Captain Newman, after the two Matabele Rebellions of 1893 and 1896, and the death of his wife, gave a general Power of Attorney to his stepson, Pat Holl, and a Power of Attorney to Messrs. Scott & Buckland, Solicitors, to sell stands in Newmansford, a property of one hundred and three acres, granted him by the British South Africa Company, for services rendered to them. He then went as Reuter's Special War Correspondent to the Russo-Jap war of 1903-4, where he disappeared, and was never heard of again.

It was in the year 1894 that Pat decided to follow his mother and go further north, to the country beyond the Limpopo, where the first Matabele Rebellion was in force. This journey he undertook on his own, on a bicycle from Ladysmith to Bulawayo. The distance from Ladysmith in the Eastern Cape to Bulawayo in the New Colony of Rhodesia, was a great challenge, through wild country, torn by war, mountainous in parts, with wide rivers and ravines, very few roads, and teeming with wild game of every species. In the Transvaal, Pat met the Zeederbergs, based in Johannesburg, who ran a coach service to the far north. A story is told of how he made a wager with them that he would reach Bulawayo before they could, and he won his bet by a good margin.

Pat became involved in the Second Matabele War, also known as the *Matabele Rebellion* or part of what is known in Zimbabwe as the First Chimurenga fought between 1896 and 1897 in the area then known as Rhodesia, now Zimbabwe. It pitted the British South Africa Company against the *amaNdebele (Matabele)* people that led to conflict with the Shona people. He joined the Artillery Regiment. He was a Bisley shot and an excellent marksman, a feat for which he was awarded a medal which he never collected.

CHAPTER 3

The Spoil of War

WHEN THE WAR ended and peace was proclaimed, for his service in the Rebellion, Pat was given in about the year 1900, a large fertile portion of virgin land in Essexvale, Umzingwane District. He named the farm Springvale.

Before Pat started farming on his own, and to build up some necessary capital he decided to work for Col. W. Napier at his farm called, SPRINGS, which was close to Springvale Farm. The Rorkes' whose forebears were famous for their part in the Zulu Rebellion, the Havners' and the Richardsons who were related to Thomas Meikle, hotel and store owners, were near neighbours and friends. To make it a viable venture, Pat purchased the adjoining land near Rorke's property, and also bought Napier's surplus, totaling in all, some eleven thousand, one hundred and forty acres.

He also sold the stands in Newmansford, property left to him by his stepfather Captain Charles Newman, to raise additional capital. It was a beautiful area, with rolling hills and valleys, rivers with plentiful water, excellent grazing, and good soils. He set to work as soon as he could, and burnt his own bricks, then built his house, and a great barn-like shed along one side, and store-rooms and outbuildings.

It was about this time that Pat, searching for companionship, took a black woman from the notable amaNdebele tribe of the Mkwananzi clan as his wife. Rhodesia was just emerging as a colony and undoubtedly there was a relative shortage of white women. So, although the taking of a black woman as a wife was relatively rare, many white men were fairly open about their liaisons.

The liaison between Pat and uMsoli Mkwananzi took place sometime in 1901 or 1902. At this time the Colony's administration system was in its infancy and would not, as a matter of principle, register a union between a black and a white person.

Mhabahaba Mkwananzi's eldest son was Dliso Mkwananzi who could not father an heir. A vaRemba inyanga (or witchdoctor) provided herbal treatment until uMasuku, his senior wife, conceived and gave birth to uMajinkila. uMajinkila had more than one wife. He fathered Alison Mkwananzi and several sons and daughters which included uSifuka and uMsoli.

Alison Mkwananzi, who was earmarked to become Chief Ngungumbane, was sent to Tiger Kloof School which was founded by the London Missionary Society at the Moffat Mission in Kuruman. Whilst Alison was at Tiger Kloof Dliso died and Majinkila was appointed Regent until 1922 when Alison returned to take up his appointment as Chief Ngungumbane.

According to the story told to me by uMsoli, and corroborated by uMagigwana, her half-brother and my father's uncle, shortly after the 1896 conflict had ended and peace restored, Pat became great friends with Majinkila Mkwananzi. He was a regular visitor at Intuta Village at eMalungwane. It was during this period of friendship that uMsoli was given to Pat as a bride.

After a short period of courtship, a wedding ceremony, according to the Ndebele custom, was performed and great quantities of millet beer were consumed. At this ceremony, uMsoli wore a very colourful traditional Ndebele wedding dress and was accompanied by a retinue of beautifully adorned brides' maids. Pat gave an unspecified number of cattle to Majinkila as a bride price or *lobola*.

Pat and uMsoli had four children. They were, Sonti, (born 1904) who was the eldest followed by Benjamin, (born 1906) Gem (born 1908) and Ruth also known as Yose (born 1910). The four siblings lived with their parents as a family.

Voluntary registration of Non-African births started in 1891 but it was not until 1893 that the first registration took place in Salisbury. However, from 1st April 1904 birth registrations became compulsory for Non-Africans; Coloured people were classified as Non-Africans at that time. For some inexplicable reason, Harry Patrick Holl did not take advantage of the facilities provided for compulsory registration. As a result, Patrick's four Coloured children were never registered.

UMsoli had persuaded Pat to build her a couple of huts close by where she could live in accordance with the tradition of the amaNdebele people. The children would often spend their time moving between the main house and their mother's huts, spending more time with their mother as Pat was often busy on the farm. Their early childhood was a very happy one as they were in a settled environment. Little did they realize how soon their lives would change?

The colonial era did not readily embrace or look kindly at interracial relationships. In the colonialists' view or perception Black and Coloured people were inferior and were often referred to as "Kaffir". Blacks or natives too, had derogatory terms for Coloured folk. The *Ndebeles* would often address Coloured children as "Ikiwa!" meaning "white person" while the Shonas would address them as "Murungu dondo!" which meant "a bush white person". These terms were intended to be derogatory and hurtful.

With the excellent grounding he had had, in the Ladysmith/Aliwal North area, and because of his enthusiasm, Pat became a very efficient mixed farmer. It was widely known and accepted by the white farming community that Pat Holl was the man who established hay-making from veldt grass in Rhodesia and was the first farmer in the country to grow wheat. He made the most wonderful sausages and bacon, - nothing can compare with them today, and his butter was always above first- grade, and was highly sought after. He was a member of the Bulawayo Agricultural Society, winning top prizes for his maize, wheat and other products, - and he was a man who had achieved his goal in life.

His dairy was unique and was built on leveled ground, on the side of a small hill. It was double-storied. The underground cellar-section was kept as cold as the cold rooms of today, by his ingenious method of gauged windows, which faced into a wide channel, cut into the side of the hill on its downward slope, to allow cool breezes from the prevailing winds to blow into the channel, and circulate the entire building, both downstairs and upstairs, to keep the whole place damp always.

The thatched upper story, level with the outside ground, had a stairway through a trap-door, down into the cool cellar, where whole sides of smoked bacon and hams home-cured by Pat, were kept, hanging in cheese-cloth bags.

This was done twice yearly; at the start, and halfway through winter.

The wooden butter churn, which was imported from Denmark, was shaped like a wide shallow basin, about two feet in diameter. By a series of cogs and teeth, the basin was rotated on its spindle and, at the same time, working the "arm" holding the "pats" which beat the cream into butter.

Pat also built cattle kraals. He ring-fenced and padlocked his farm. He established a small herd of dairy cattle for the dairy. His livestock included beef cattle, sheep, pigs, and the usual poultry, including ducks and turkeys.

Finally, he built a large dam to irrigate winter wheat, using the "channel and flood" method, and planted a large orchard, with all the citrus fruits, as well as apples, peaches, greengage plums and nectarines. He also grew his own coffee, and what a wonderful aroma there was, when he roasted the beans.

On the farm, there was always a great deal of odd jobs and, sometimes unusual work that a farmer must do. Pat was interested in iron-work. There was no electricity or welding machine in those days, but he had a wonderful smithy shop, with a Forge and a huge bellows, on which his little children used to swing up and down to keep the forge fire burning brightly, always while he was busy working there. He was even a first-class cobbler and repaired boots and shoes, when needed, on strange looking three legged "lasts" with different sole and heel sizes.

How did Pat achieve all this on his own, you may ask, seeing that he never trained as an artisan? There was no task that he would tackle that was not done properly, - and he could do anything! He was competent in all types of work an artisan does, including trades such as bricklaying
and plastering, carpentry and any other manual job.

One of Pat's greatest abilities was his handling of snakes which he would catch and send to the Port Elizabeth Snake Park in the Eastern Cape. Pat had a knack of holding a python at the base of its head, to prevent it from constricting. This feat always amazed and thrilled his friends.

One incident of special note made headline news in the local Bulawayo Chronicle. A farm-hand reported that he had seen a very large python disappearing down an ant-bear hole. Pat went to investigate. Taking a grain bag and a lantern with him and, being held by the legs, he crawled into the ant-bear hole, head first, and managed to get the python into the bag after which he was pulled out. This python measured over 20 feet.

On another occasion, he amazed two visitors by catching a python in the open veldt which had just been reported to him by one of the farm workers. Whether Pat was ever paid for these snakes is not known, but they were well accepted.

CHAPTER 4

The Winds of Change

PAT HAD BEEN FARMING for a little over ten years, when he met a lovely young widow, Genevieve Paula Blazina. She had a baby son and his name was René. Genevieve Paula Bailley was born in St. Cloud, Paris on the 28th December 1889.

Her mother was the young daughter of a French Noble Family, who fell in love with her Tutor, a young man of Scots and French parentage, named Pierre Bailley. He taught her English and she secretly married him. When it was discovered, however, her parents had the marriage annulled as she was under age, and Pierre was banished. Because of the two-young people's love for one another, a baby girl was born, and she was named Genevieve Paula Bailey. In France in those days, most marriages, births and deaths were registered in the church where the event took place, and with the state France was in after the earlier wars, and the turmoil of the Russo-Jap War of 1903-4, and the First Great World War, so much in France was destroyed.

Pierre loved his little daughter, and he kept in contact with her over the years. After her preliminary schooling, and when he was able, and she was old enough, he took her and her nurse-duenna, named Maria Cariosi, as far away as he could from France, to Africa. They eventually arrived in the New Colony of Rhodesia, sometime in 1904. When Genevieve was in her fifteenth year she completed her education at the Convent school, and then took oral French classes in the school. Pierre had opened up a very exclusive French Restaurant, with rented-out overnight accommodation, and he catered for the businessmen and the more affluent farmers, when they came to town, and it was here that Pat met the lovely young widow.

She had married a tall young Austrian, from the Austrian-Serb Border, by the name of Philippe Blazina, who, like so many other venturesome young men of that day, had come to Africa for excitement. There, he met Genevieve, and there was keen competition between this extremely handsome, and elegant young man, and a young British Police Officer, by the name of Meredith-known as Jack, who taught her riding. But Philip won her love, and their wedding took place on the 6th September 1906, when she was seventeen and a half years old, and he was twenty-three.

Her father had married Maria Cariosi, to her dismay, on 8th August, the previous year, and she could not accept or approve of the marriage.

Two years later, tragedy struck Genevieve. It was a very distressing time, and the years-1908 and 1909 were a very unhappy period in her life. Her dearly loved father had died suddenly from malaria complications, just three years after his marriage, followed by the death of her baby daughter from meningitis, and then a year later, on the 4th of March 1909, by the death of her young husband, from Black Water Fever Suppression, at the age of twenty-six years, when her baby son René was only six months old. One cannot begin to imagine how she coped with her sorrow.

Maria, who had now become Genevieve's stepmother, continued to run the Restaurant, with the aid of the French Master-Chef, Pierre Paul Moudreay, who had been with the business since its inception, and whom she eventually married. Pierre had a son from his previous marriage, named Frederique, and a cousin by the name of Margaret, an extremely plain woman. After the death of her husband, Genevieve and her baby son had no option but to live at the Restaurant, with Maria, whom she disliked more than ever since her second marriage. She was unhappy until she met Pat Holl.

It was at Maria Cariosi's Restaurant that Pat met Genevieve on one of his regular visits whenever he was in town. Pat was absolutely smitten with her, and after a short courtship, they were married on the 10th June 1910. He took her and little René to England for their honey-moon, and a six-month holiday to meet his family still living there, leaving the farm in the care of friends, and the farm Manager.

It was whilst on his honeymoon in England that Pat made up his mind to put away his Black wife and his three Coloured children. On his return from England, he decided to send uMsoli back to her father's village in nearby *Malungwane*. No doubt such a fateful decision may have been influenced by his new wife.

Sometime in the summer of 1910, uMsoli and her four children left Springvale farm by ox-wagon laden with goods, including groceries and a large herd of cattle which was intended to be the children's inheritance, for their new home in Malungwane. Judging from Pat's reaction to Sonti and Gem, two of his Coloured children that came to see him some time later in 1915, it had been his hope that the cattle would be used by uMsoli to educate the children as well as being their inheritance. When the siblings left Springvale, Sonti was about 6, Ben 4, Gem 2 and Ruth 3 months old.

Unfortunately, uMsoli, like most of the native or black women of her time, had no education and, therefore, did not understand or appreciate the value and importance of sending her children to school. When she left Springvale farm she did not realize what impact the move would have on the future of her children and her children's children.

Speaking with my grandmother, many years later, she told me, on several occasions that Pat had wanted to build a home for her and her children, following their break-up, some distance away on the eleven thousand acre farm; far from his residence, but she had refused his offer. She had refused his offer, perhaps, through pride, jealousy, anger or disappointment. Had my grandmother accepted his offer the outcome for the four siblings may have been different?

On arrival at their new home at Intuta Village at eMalungwane, uMsoli's father, Majinkila, directed that the children be placed under the care or supervision of uMsoli's brother, uSifuka Mkwananzi in accordance with the Ndebele custom, who would exercise control over the cattle as Trustee. In practical terms, however, this meant that he had total control over them and on the use of the cattle.

It is pertinent to point out at this juncture, that uMsoli and uSifuka had the same biological father but different mothers. In effect Sifuka was uMsoli's half- brother.

Not long after her arrival at eMalungwane with her four children, my grandmother, uMsoli, left Intuta village to get married and moved to live in Avoca, which is situated south of the Filabusi Administrative centre, leaving the children behind. Because of the mother's decision to leave her children behind, they lost their inheritance from their father.

As a result, none of the children, except the youngest, Ruth, were able to get an education.

Growing up in the Intuta village in eMalungwane was very traumatic and challenging to the children who had been accustomed to living with Pat and their mother. They longed to return to Springvale to be united with their father but soon realised the futility of their wish.

In the summer of 1915, Sonti and Gem left eMalungwane to visit their father, Pat, and travelled through the bush to Springvale Farm, a journey of about 8 miles. On arrival, they went over to the workers' housing and spoke to the Native Farm Assistant whom they knew. On seeing the girls and knowing that it would be inappropriate to take them over to the house where Genevieve was, he decided to go over alone and call Pat to come over to the compound.

Pat came over to meet with them and in isiNdebele; he asked them, "Why are you not in school?" for they were both of school going age and it was school season and they should have been at school.

"Because there's no one to send us to school" Sonti replied sadly, "they are saying that there is no money to buy clothes and pay school fees" she continued".

"What has happened to the cattle that I sent you with?" he asked with deep concern.

"The cattle are there but we are not getting any benefit from them. Our mother has left us and gone to live in Filabusi and is married to another man" she replied with tears streaming down her cheeks. "We are suffering. We are made to work in the fields planting maize and other crops the whole day. We are treated as slaves."

At this point Pat broke down and wept. "Shall I send you back with some more cattle?" he asked.

"What is the use" they cried, "they will just keep them for themselves and nothing will change" she replied.

The meeting ended. He arranged for them to get some food, packed some provisions, gave them some money and had them escorted to the Intuta Village promising that he would do something about getting them to go to school.

Archival records indicate that Pat did take steps to set up a Guardians Fund for his Coloured children. However, it would seem, his efforts were blocked or frustrated, possibly by those who were opposed to the idea. Years later, when I asked René after we met at Phyllis Lewis' house in Avondale,

Harare, he told me that there were documents relating to this issue that were in a hut that caught fire. It appears that the hut in question was deliberately set alight to prevent the Fund from taking effect. He did not elaborate further on the matter.

When Sonti and Gem returned after visiting their father at Springvale, their brother, Ben, asked them how their father was and what was the outcome of their visit?

"We spoke to Pat, but he was not able to help us", Sonti retorted with tears in her eyes, "the only thing he did was to cry and offer to send more cattle," she continued, "but I told him that sending more cattle would not solve our situation". They also told Ben that they had seen Pat's white children but did not get to know their names. "There were three boys and one girl. They seemed happy and contented unlike us" they concluded.

Ben could not hide his frustration and disappointment. He thought about how his life had been and how it had now completely changed since leaving Springvale farm a few years back. He was 9 years old now and was not able to go to school like some of the children in the village. One of his cousins was going to school at Tiger Kloof in South Africa and was being groomed to become the next chief Mkwananzi. His fees were sometimes raised from the slaughter of the cattle that had come from his father. When he had asked his uncle about himself and his three sisters going to school he was told that there was no money to pay their school fees.

He often thought of Pat and could not understand why he had not arranged for him and his sisters to attend school. Sometimes he would daydream and imagine himself back at Springvale surrounded by his native friends that he had left behind. "He hates us", he thought, "He hates us because we are not white like his other children". "If only our mother was white things would have been different", he concluded.

Since arriving at eMalungwane his daily chores had been to rise early every morning to open the cattle kraal and take the cattle to pasture; returning later in the day and, sometimes in the evening. During the plowing season he would take turns with the other boys in the village to plough the fields and carry out other chores as necessary. It was very hard and back-breaking work and he did this for many years that followed.

Sonti, Gem and Ruth were given roles according to their ages which included cooking, planting, collecting wood, harvesting, collecting water from the well/borehole/ river and cleaning. These chores were carried out throughout their stay at eMalungwane until they got married. Sonti married a man named Cele and went to live in the Victoria Falls area of Matabeleland. She bore seven children and their names were Orpah, Thule, Welcome, Rachel, Aggripa, Rhodes and Priscilla.

Gem married a man named Kunene Ndhlela and had three children by him. Their names were Abel, Aleki and Jane. It is not clear how her marriage to Mr. Ndhlela ended. It is quite possible that he may have died. She later married a Mr. Ngwenya and had four children by him and their names were Mthandazo, Martha, Biti and Diana.

Ruth was able to go to school at Hope Fountain Mission where she later became a teacher. It was while she was attending Hope Fountain Mission that she met, fell in love and married a man by the name of Thomas Mazinyane, who was also a teacher. She bore five children and their names were Maggie, Esther, Napoleon, Churchill and Alice. They lived on their farm not far from Solusi Mission and near Figtree.

CHAPTER 5

Lost Inheritance

WORLD WAR 1, also known as First World War broke out on 28 July 1914. When the idea of an African unit to fight under the British flag was raised in colonial administrative circles, it was meant to be recruited primarily from the Ndebele ethnic group. The reason for this initial emphasis on the Ndebele originated with the rather romantic European perception of that group, well established in literature by that time, as having inherent warrior-like traits. Historically, the Ndebele had a common history with the Zulu, supposedly the most warlike African group which had fought their way north in the early nineteenth century under the famous warrior–king Mzilikazi. Of the first five hundred recruits, three hundred came from Matabeleland, the predominantly Ndebele region of the colony.

After the war ended on 11 November 1918, the Ndebele chiefs, including Regent Chief Majinkila Mkwananzi, prepared a lavish feast in honour of those returning home from the war. Ben's uncle, without consulting or even informing him, slaughtered an ox, which had been his favourite animal, as part of the village's contribution to the grand feast.

It was widely known and acknowledged that the cattle belonged to Harry Patrick Holl's Coloured children with uMsoli. Benjamin, being the only boy was expected to take possession of the cattle on attaining adulthood. Ben was only about 13 years old at that time. He was angry and disappointed. Without saying goodbye, he left Intuta Village at eMalungwane and went to Avoca where he had heard that his mother was living with her new husband and son. Up until now he had been hoping and expecting he would be given his cattle when he became of age.

He had no money, so he travelled on foot sleeping on the way. Finally, he arrived in Avoca. He was warmly received by his mother, step-father and his half-brother aged about 4 years, by the name of Mahumuchana. As no one had bothered to look for him he remained in this area of Filabusi for many years and witnessed the birth and growth of his second half-brother, Reuben.

Whilst living in Avoca Ben became acquainted with most of the Coloured people living at eNkankezi during the nineteen years that he remained in Filabusi. Many of the folk in this settlement became his friends. eNkankezi was popularly known as Chimpken's farm or koMafuta. There were very few Coloured homes when Ben first arrived at Avoca in 1918. However, by the time he left the area in 1940 or 1941 there had been a significant influx of Coloured people who had come from all the regions of Matabeleland South and, even from far-off places such as Kezi.

Mr. Chimpken had a store on his farm. The store was popularly referred to as "koMafuta". This was because Mr. Chimpken was rotund. The store was on the left side of the road from Bulawayo to Shabani. Some of the families that I can remember, which my father befriended and was well acquainted with, were the Reids, the Ambroses, the Johnsons, the Weales, the Bells and the Kennedys – all children of settlers.

Mr. Chimpken himself had Coloured children. I often thought the reason for his concern for the welfare of Coloured people was because he had Coloured children. Unlike Harry Patrick Holl he sent his children to school to get an education. Most of the children born to white settlers and native women at that time had no place to go or land on which to build a home. Many had come to Mr. Chimpken who gave them sanctuary, places to build houses, plant crops and rear cattle at a nominal annual rental. I have often thought that, maybe, Chimpken was acting on behalf of the colonial settler regime.

Coloured women at that time were few. This may explain why Ben may not have been able to find a woman to marry from amongst the Coloured community of eNkankezi. Instead, he sought to marry a woman from the local Ndebele community.

In September 1928 Ben received word that his father had been killed in a shooting accident on his farm. He was told that the accident occurred whilst his father was checking the gun traps that he had set to kill reed-buck, and other vermin, that were destroying his crops. Although he hardly knew his father he felt some loss and sadness about his death.

In 1938 Ben met and fell in love with uMathoso Dhlamini. She was from the Dhlamini clan and a descendant of King Sobhuza 1 (also known as Ngwane IV, Somhlolo) who was king of Swaziland from 1815 to 1836. Mathoso already had her own child out of wedlock whom she had named Kathleen, born in 1937 but Ben did not mind that for he loved her dearly. Their marriage took place in Bokodo, Filabusi, in April 1938. They had a traditional Swazi wedding called umtsimba whereby the bride commits herself to her new family for the remainder of her life. It was a colourful ceremony which lasted a few days. He built a beautiful home for his family not far from his parents' home.

Whilst living at Avoca, three children were born to Ben and uMathoso – one girl and two boys. The first boy died in infancy. The surviving children were Ava and Steven. This brought the total number of children in the home to three including Kathleen.

With a young and growing family of three children, life became somewhat difficult as the income from growing crops and doing odd jobs in the neighbourhood was insufficient to clothe and feed the family. Vigorous efforts to get his cattle from Sifuka proved fruitless as he consistently met with deceit and empty promises. Because he lacked education and, combined with the fact that he was Coloured, it was impossible for him to get legal assistance to make a claim against his uncle Sifuka.

Ben began to look for employment in the nearby mines but met with no success. Without any education at all, the odds of finding a job were heavily stacked against him. It would have been easier to find a job if he was a native but with his light-brown complexion he could not find a job even as a laborer. In desperation, Ben started to extend his search for jobs farther afield in places like Belingwe and Shabani. Finally, he got a job in Shabani at the Shabanie Asbestos Mine as a Hoist Driver. This was indeed a great relief to him.

At that time racism and bigotry were deeply entrenched in the colonial system. White mine workers were housed in beautiful houses with large gardens.

Blacks or native employees, as they were then called, were housed in compounds which were comprised of densely populated houses with communal amenities such as communally shared bathrooms and latrines.

With his family living in Avoca this meant he had to travel to Avoca at the end of every month in order to bring money and provisions to the family. Not only was this inconvenient; it was both tiring and expensive to commute. The family decided it would be best to find a place where Ben could build a suitable home for the family.

Ben started his employment with the Shabanie Asbestos Mine early in 1940. Although allocated a house in the native compound of Nil Mine he did not feel comfortable living there. He decided to rent a piece of land at Mabula Farm in *Dadaya*; some 12 miles from Shabani.

The land belonged to the new Dadaya Mission and was administered by Sir Reginald Stephen Garfield Todd, who was born on 13 July 1908 and died 13 October 2002 and his wife Grace. Garfield Todd, as leader of the United Rhodesia Party, later became a Liberal Prime Minister of Sothern Rhodesia from 1953 to 1958. When white rule was later introduced by Ian Douglas Smith and his Rhodesia Front Party, he became an opponent of white minority rule in Rhodesia.

CHAPTER 6

Life at Springvale

AFTER UMSOLI LEFT with her Coloured children, Pat brought his new wife to live at Springvale Farm. Over the years, ten children were born to Pat and Genevieve (fondly known as Gene), amongst whom were twins, and with the oldest René, born 13 September 1908, there were eleven in the family. The ten children were, Harry Cecil, born 20 March 1911, William Vere, born 17 August 1913, Ida Florence, born 30 April 1914, Lucy Lorna, born 16 March 1915, Alice Mary, born 17 December 1917, Eric Patrick and Mona Frances, born 19 January 1920, Phyllis Patricia, born 2 April 1921,
Evelyn Theresa, born 6 July 1923, and John Clifford, born 3 June 1926.

It was a happy, full and carefree life on beautiful Springvale. The children felt that theirs was the whole world, and that nothing of worth existed outside Springvale.

Schooling began on the farm. A special school room was built, and tutors from England were employed. First was a Mr. Hobbs, later followed by a Mr. Harwood, then a Miss Phillips, and finally a Mr. Faulks who was nicknamed "Mr. Fox" by the twins. There was also a nurse-maid, a Miss Winnie, to help with the care of the smaller children. This continued until boarding-school age.

On special occasions, the younger children could join their parents, and the older members of the family for the main meal of the day, but the children had to be on their best behaviour, freshly washed faces and hands and hair neatly brushed. They were taught good table manners and were not encouraged to talk at meals when with grown-ups. Pat would tell them that they should always leave the table feeling that they could eat one more slice of bread. There was always grace before and after meals which was said by Pat.

As Springvale was only seventeen miles from Bulawayo, there were always crowds of visitors and friends, coming out for picnics or for long weekends and for holiday breaks. Even though the family was so large, children from the children's schools, whose homes were too distant for the shorter and long-weekends, would be encouraged to stay with the family. As a result, there were delightful times spent camping at Fern *Spruit and Jobbers Spruit*, two of the most popular picnic sites that were always frequented. This was apart from the lovely dam, always with abundant clear water, to swim and splash in.

The rivers at Springvale, and in most of that part of Matabeleland, were deep and high banked, with groves of large Mimosa thorn trees, and other riverine trees, a breathtaking sight in spring when in bloom, with their lovely yellow flowers, and exquisite scent. Most rivers in Matabeleland, though beautiful in their own way, were wide and flat, with great stretches of sand, and dry, apart from occasional rocky pools here and there, but which could become impassible in wet weather, except where the main bridges crossed them. In those early years, the bridges on the main routes were low-level, and in the remoter areas, there were none at all, causing travellers to be held up for days at a time.

At about this time, Pat bought his first car, a shining dark, blue- green American canvas-topped Ford Saloon, which he learned to drive. The vehicle was mainly used for journeys to town, and to take children to school instead of using the train from Maguga Halt station which was located on the farm, or, as previously, by horse and trap.

René was a tease and was the bane of both Ida's and Alice's lives, but Lucy would just laugh at him, and would calmly shrug her shoulders and he would get no joy out of her. Ida always took the bait, and would rant and rave, and shout "Oh mummy, look at René", and he would reply "Aren't I pretty" in a sing-song voice. Alice would fly into a tantrum and throw things at him. There was a night that she "ran away", no doubt, just to punish him, and how Pat and the boys took lanterns to search for her, and there she was, sitting on a rock by the duck-pond, on the river which fed the dam.

It appears that Ivy may have been the instigator of René's mischievousness. She was a young girl, nine years René's senior, whom Pat had brought out from England. It was his intention to get someone as a companion-help for his wife, whilst they were overseas. Ivy was the daughter of a neighbour of a family friend in England, and she suffered from Asthma. It was urgent that she should live in a warm, dry climate; so, Patrick was persuaded to bring her to Rhodesia. Being twelve years old, she was sent to school to finish her education, and become part of the family.

She was a mischievous young scamp, and full of fun, but she was to become the life and soul of the party, and she led René into all sorts of scrapes. Phyllis remembered years later, her recalling an episode she had with the farm manager, a Mr. Jeffreys, a rather simple man, and how he roared at her. One afternoon, when no one was near, she cut a small branch of mimosa thorns, and carefully put it into his bed, under the bedclothes, and gleefully awaited his return after a day's hard work, to watch him flop down for a moment's respite. This seemed to amuse her greatly, and she would double up with laughter, until he chased her.

It was through her, sometime later, that Mr. Jeffreys and Margaret Moudray were married. She had mischievously written two notes of proposal, from one to the other, which they obviously thought were genuine, gladly accepting each other's proposal. Their marriage turned out well, fortunately, and they had four children.

René had attended St. George's College, while the college was still in Bulawayo. He was an excellent Boxer, and he was the college's Captain. He was the unbeatable Heavy-Weight Champion in the inter-schools boxing Championships, and an all-rounder in athletics, winning the one-hundred yards, the two hundred yards, the quarter mile, and the half mile. He was also the Inter-Schools Champion at Putting-the-shot, and Pole-vaulting. For his prowess in all sports and also his academic work, he was awarded the *Victor Ludorum*, and was Pat's pride and joy, being the keen sportsman, he was.

Harry, known as Buster at school, also attended St. George's College in Bulawayo. Like René, he was a natural, both in sports and schoolwork, but he was inclined to be lazy and his best was never that important to him, as long as he was comparatively equal to other boys. These maybe because he was inclined to be shy, especially of the female gender. René always maintained that Buster was an excellent boxer, and very good to watch, and the only way he could get Buster to do well, was to tell his opponent to go for the face, especially the nose, knowing full well what the result would be. A punch on the nose would be a red flag to a bull, and within minutes his opponent would be floored and out for a count.

Billy was also a top sportsman, but unlike Buster, he was not shy, and always gave of his best, both academically and in the sports field. He went to the college in Bulawayo, until the school moved to Salisbury, where he completed his education. He was very popular at school with the other boys, and also with Masters, and excelled in Cricket and Hockey.

Pat would never miss any sports event his sons took part in, whether it is athletics, cricket, rugby or boxing, and one can see today, in the Salisbury St. George's College archives, what excellent sportsmen the Holl boys were. Eric is particularly remembered there today as one of the finest head boys, the college had. He was also Victor Ludorum and an excellent all-rounder in his senior years. It was many years later that Pat's youngest son, John Clifford, attended St. George's College, after Pat's death. He was a lovely boxer to watch, and his sister Phyllis recounted a contest held in Bulawayo, that she attended with her mum. His clean technique was a real pleasure to watch, and he won his match on points.

Ida and Billy were always very close, and she joined him in so many of their adventures on the farm. One story Phyllis recalled and which she thought well worth relating, was a "tall fish story…" It was during school holidays and Harry and Bill, who had been given fishing rods for Christmas, decided to go down to the river where the dam wall was built, to catch fish for supper. Ida, having no rod, said she would make her own rod and follow later. Her rod was a length of a slim bamboo, her line a few feet of string, and her hook an open safety pin. Sometime later she was ready and accompanied by "Skip", the woolly Airedale, she made her way to the fishing site.

The boys had been fishing without any luck for over an hour and were becoming hot and restless. They had used as bait, worms, legs of frogs they had slaughtered, bits of dicky-birds they had shot, and even lumps of *sadza*, all without any success, and only decided to try a little longer, to give Ida a chance. "Skip" was lying beside her and she spied a fully engorged tick on his neck. She removed it, pierced it on to her safety pin hook, and cast her rod into the water. Within half an hour, she had caught three lovely big breams, to the amazement of her brothers, using the same tick, which by now was just a bit of membrane. This was the beginning of her lifelong love for fishing.

Billy's special hobby was collecting birds' eggs and he had a lovely selection. Ida always accompanied him, especially on these occasions, and sometimes Lucy, who was still very young. Billy loved birds and tried never to disturb them. He would very carefully take only one egg from a nest, pass it to Ida and she would carefully put it into a little basket she carried for this purpose. Then would begin the job of sorting them out, blowing the contents clear, and labeling them. Billy would also shoot for the "pot", when Pat was too busy to do so.

Harry could never bring himself to shoot for the "pot" again, after a never-to-be forgotten experience he had in his boy-hood years. He and Billy and two school friends were out shooting, and it was Harry's turn to shoot. A duiker was seen not too far away and taking careful aim, he shot it, but not quite fatally. He went up to it just as it died, and then discovered it was a female with a newly-born fawn. Most small buck, male and female, have horns, and are difficult to differentiate from a distance. This incident affected Harry greatly. He carried the fawn home, holding back his tears, nursed it to adulthood and it became a family pet and was named Peggy.

René told another buck story. Many years before, when he was still very young, he found a baby duiker, lying among some rocks, while he was out for a walk. As small as he was, he picked it up and carried it home. It was a female, and he called it Binny. She became his special pet and followed him everywhere he went. As she grew older, she could wander off, always eventually returning home, until one day she never did return, and it was surmised that she had found a mate.

Phyllis tells of another amazing incident in her very early years; she could barely have been five years old. The family had all gone picnicking one day at Malangwani – a river that fed the dam. Pat was busy on the farm.

On the river bank, there were the most beautiful trees which over hung the water. Many picnics were held there, and the older children spent their time climbing on the trees and jumping into the water.

It was a lovely day, and Alice, Eric and Mona were playing around in the shallow pools. The boys and their school pals were diving into the deeper water from overhanging branches, when Ida and Lucy decided to follow suit. That is when it happened… Lucy did not emerge. Chaos! Within seconds, their mother, who could not swim, jumped into the water fully clothed, leaving baby

Cliff and Eve with Phyllis to keep an eye on them, on the river bank. It seemed ages before Genevieve eventually emerged with Lucy half-conscious in her arms. What a brave mother she was.

Mona and Eric were little imps when they started school on the farm. They had a Miss Phillips for the first two terms. During the time she was with them, they had to be separated from each other, as far away as the bench would allow, as they had a naughty habit of tickling each other and bursting into giggles. At other times they would take it in turns, and ask to be excused, and would run down to the duck-pond to play. This was very soon discovered, reported to Dad, and stopped once she got wise to their tricks. But what joy it was to them both, when school closed for the holidays. During the middle of the second term, they settled down, and stopped the tickling game.

For the third term, a Mr. Faulkes, whom they named "Mr. Fox", was their Tutor as it was decided that they needed a man's strong discipline. Their new game by now was pulling awful faces at each other, at which Eric was an expert. While Mr. Fox was busy at the board one morning, he was confronted by Mona, making the most dreadful face at Eric, who had been called to the front to recite something, and which had caused him to burst into laughter. This was in retaliation of the face which he had previously pulled at her. For punishment, Mona was made to stand on one leg in the corner, facing the wall. However, soon after this incident, they behaved themselves, and settled down to their schoolwork. They were very bright, and learnt quickly, and were above average in reading, writing and arithmetic, and quite ready for Boarding-School the following year. It was thanks to Lucy that the younger children were able to read long before their school years. The three youngest members of the family did not have tuition on the farm, but went to the Convent as boarders, as they had their older sisters there to keep an eye on them.

Mona told of this incident which remained indelible in her mind.
It happened when her father took the children for a picnic, and for some fishing, to the river by the dam. It must have taken place during the school term as none of the older children were present, and by this time Alice had also gone to boarding school. Eric and Mona had just turned five, Phyllis was there, and Eve was eighteen months old, and was sitting on her mother's lap.

CHAPTER 7

The Accident at Springvale

PAT HAD BEEN troubled by reed and other small buck breaking into the wheat fields and destroying his crops. The wheat was being grown under irrigation, and in order to save as much of it as possible, he was in the habit of setting spring-guns to destroy the vermin.

On Wednesday night, 6 September 1928, he set two guns facing one another, and then returned to his home.

During the evening, however, he heard one of these explode. He proceeded with his wife, Genevieve, and a native, who was his boss-boy, to the trap, where he found a buck shot dead. He was in the act of reloading the discharged weapon when, for some unaccountable reason, the opposite gun went off, killing him instantly.

Mrs. Holl was wounded by the same charge, while the native also received part of the shot or pellet in the body. Pat lived long enough to ask Mrs. Holl if she was alright.

Mr. Jones, the Native Commissioner at Umzingwane, was sent for immediately and he took Mr. and Mrs. Holl and the native to hospital in Bulawayo without delay.

Pat died on the way to hospital. Mrs. Holl, however, was found to be not seriously injured although she was detained in hospital pending an X-Ray Examination. Mrs. Holl had been shot in the side and back and hospitalized for three months.

Pat was given a full Pioneer Funeral, and the Cortege Procession of cars following the coffin was one of the longest seen in Bulawayo at that time.

Pat was very popular and well-liked. He was a great loss to his family, friends and the whole farming community.

Genevieve continued farming at Springvale with the help of various farm managers for two years, but the loss of animal stock and produce was more than she could bear; so, eventually she decided to lease the farm on a percentage basis.

Genevieve and her family moved into town. René had completed his education before Pat's death and had joined the Department of Internal Affairs as Junior Native commissioner. At the time of Pat's death, he was stationed at Wankie.

It was a very sad time for the family, as they left the farm by Ox-Wagon, laden with goods to catch the train at Maguga Halt. Tearfully, the younger children called out, "goodbye house, goodbye cattle kraals, goodbye mealie-lands, goodbye everything" as they neared the Halt. The family was fortunate, however, as they were able to visit the farm over long weekends. Over school holidays, they had the privilege to visit with the Havners who were special friends.

As a young farmer's wife, Genevieve had had to learn the art of bread making. Her initial attempts were somewhat disastrous but with patience and the encouragement of Pat she became an expert as time went by, gaining top prizes for all her baking in the Bulawayo Agricultural Shows.

Now that she lived in town, she continued to make bread for the family; the aroma of baking bread would attract friends from all around the area.

Ida was enrolled at the Convent school. She was one of the most mischievous girls at the Convent. Years later, when she attended an "Old Girls'" Reunion Dinner, and met the school's Principal, Sister Concillia, she was told her escapades had added "spice" to their otherwise uneventful lives.

At one time she furiously attacked a nun on Sports Duty, for daring to pull Lucy off the Hockey-Field, by her thick hair, while playing hockey with her black stockings rolled down, during a match against an opposing school, as she full well knew the reason for this. Lucy had tripped, and her stockings were knee less.

One of her other escapades was the time that she paraded as a nun. This happened at night, after nine o'clock, when the seniors came in from night study. Ida had previously been punished and had been demoted to the junior dormitory for one week. The matron-in-charge, who slept in the junior dormitory and behind a cubicle, had already gone to bed, and all was quiet. She placed her disrobed habit and veil, etc., over the cubicle railing.

Ida, in a daring mood, carefully took each garment down, and robed herself in them, then; boldly she walked through the nun's quarters, out into the school grounds, where several nuns were walking in pairs, which was the rule, reciting their prayers and rosaries.

Ida walked around, greeting and bowing as she passed each couple, to their astonishment, as she was alone. After circling the grounds, she calmly returned through their quarters, to the dormitory, where she undressed, replacing the garments, and went to bed. No-one ever enquired as to who the mysterious nun was.

Another of Ida's stories was the time she missed benediction and was reported to the Principal. When asked why she did not attend, she simply replied that she had left her hat in the classroom and was not allowed in church without a head covering. When asked why she had not borrowed a hat, she calmly said, "Oh no Sister, my father always told me never to use anyone's hat, as I would get "nits". She got away with it.

Lucy was a very clever girl. She was an excellent sportswoman and was captain of the Hockey and Tennis teams. She was popular, both with the teachers and other students. She grew into a beautiful young lady, quite the prettiest of all the girls in the family and had a fair share of male admirers, but her real interest at that time was her future career. She won a Rhodes scholarship, and was due to attend the University at Grahamstown.

The new family home in Bulawayo was in Main Street, which became a haven for the large family and their friends. It was here that Ida met her husband-to-be, though at the time, she had not considered that aspect of her life.

Alice had grown into a beautiful young teenager. She had always been the odd one out – too young for the five older members of the family, and too old for the five younger children. But now, with her lovely blonde looks and shapely tall figure, she attracted a large crowd of young teenagers. She had a lovely mezzo-soprano voice and would try to make Mona harmonize with her and berate her when she would slip into the wrong key.

World War II was declared in September 1939 and the boys enlisted into the Army and the Air Force. Genevieve had decided that it would be better, and safer, to move to the suburb and, accordingly, she bought a large house in the popular Bulawayo suburb where many of the pioneers and early settlers had built their lovely homes.

This move was to be one of many that she embarked on as she realised that buying and selling was becoming a profitable venture. Genevieve was a wonderful and creative gardener who, because of this, was able to add attraction to the selling price.

The six older members of our family now had full lives of their own, and the five younger children were busy growing up. Their teenage years were happy and carefree, and their home was always popular amongst all their friends. They made their own entertainment, with surprise parties over weekends, which would alternate between their home and their friends' homes.

They would go on long cycle rides to outlying picnic spots, to the very popular Matopo Hills, and nearer town to the Hillside Dam.

It was a time of fun and growing up, and the children did not lack friends of both sexes and life went on despite the war.

There were training camps for the Army and Air Force in Bulawayo, Gwelo and Salisbury, and uniformed men were seen everywhere.

It was a time of sorrow and happiness, and a time of love and marriage. Lucy had met the man she was to marry at Rhodes University, and Alice was married in Bulawayo in 1938.

In April 1941, tragedy struck the family once again. Billy was killed in an accident in Nairobi whilst on leave from his regiment, the Argyle & Sutherland Highlanders. This brought the horror of war closer to the family, and it had only just begun. Genevieve was heartbroken, and she could never accept it until the war ended and Billy did not come home.

Phyllis was the first of the younger members of the family to be married. She was nearly 20 years old when she married Tom Lewis. They were married on July 19, 1941, before Tom left for the Middle East.

Mona was married two years later in September 1943 to a young Englishman named Leslie Taylor, who was in Rhodesia with the R.A.F., and Eve, the youngest sister, was married in April 1945 to a sergeant, Leonard Vinton, an Englishman, also in the R.A.F. During the war there were many men from overseas being trained in the Rhodesian and South African training camps.

After the war ended in April 1945, all the R.A.F. contingent were repatriated back to their countries.

Both Mona, with her little year-old daughter, Erica, and Eve left Rhodesia, to join their husbands, now in England, sailing from Cape Town, towards the end of December 1945, arriving in England in mid- January 1946.

It was several years later, that Eric and Cliff were to be married. Cliff married Josephine Everest, a nurse from England, in 1952, and Eric married a South African girl named Cynthia Marsden whom he had met in Natal.

Tom Lewis, Phyllis' husband, returned home from Europe on the anniversary of the First World War's Armistice Day, 11th November 1945.
Pat and Gene's family were now scattered over the whole country, also in South Africa, and England, and a new era had begun.

Genevieve passed away on August 28, 1976, at nearly 86 years of age and she had thirty-nine grandchildren and a very large number of great-grandchildren.

CHAPTER 8

Servitude

BY THE BEGINNING of 1952, Rene' had been transferred to Filabusi. He was now the Native Commissioner for the *Insiza* District. His immediate task was to implement the Land Tenure Act. One of his first major assignments was to reallocate Africans' land in Bokodo, Filabusi to *Jotsholo* in the *Lupane* district. *Jotsholo* had poor quality soils compared to Bokodo. In addition, this area had endemic malaria as well as being infested with tsetse flies. Families were pushed out of their homes and their lands consolidated into large cattle ranches sold to a handful of white settlers. Many people at Bokodo knew Rene' as Ben's brother; so, they would approach him and complain to him bitterly; as though he was able to do anything about their demise.

Part of René's mandate was to relocate the Coloured families living on Chimpken's Farm onto 21 acres (8.5 ha) lots for purchase at *Malole* in the *Gwatemba* area. A significant number of the Coloureds, who had the means at that time, took this offer. Notable amongst them were Mr. Weale, Mr. Williams and Mr. Ambrose. Those who were not able to purchase the lots rented from those that had purchased the lots. Coloureds that remained at Chimpken's farm were evicted and the land was converted to a ranch and sold.

I was born in Shabani. My father worked for the local Mine as a Hoist Driver. Our parents, Benjamin and uMathoso (also known as *"uMadlhamini"*) had four children named Kathleen, Ava, Steven and myself. I am the fourth child. Kathleen was popularly known *"uMadade"* which was her Ndebele name.

When he joined the company in 1940 or 1941, there was no housing set aside for Coloureds and, being the only Coloured employed by the mine at that time, he was allocated a house in Nil Mine Village.

Instead of taking up a house which had been allocated to him in the African residential compound he elected to rent a piece of land at Mabula Farm and build his own house. Mabula Farm was in Dadaya, 20 miles from where he worked. I guess my father chose this option because he was accustomed to living in a rural environment.

The family was still in Dadaya when I was born at the local Mine Hospital and taken by car to Mabula Farm. I have no recollection of life at Mabula Farm, probably because the family did not reside here for long. It has never been made clear to me why we left Dadaya and came to settle in Nil Mine which was one of three African or Native residential villages owned by the mine. The reason could be that he may have lost the lease and forced by circumstances to take up free accommodation at Nil Mine.

I have been told that, on a certain day when my mother went to the well with me at her back, Garfield Todd passed by the well and noticed me. He approached my mother and enquired about me. A few days later he came to our house and asked my father and mother if he could take me away to New Zealand where I could receive an education along with his daughter, Judith, who was three years older than I was. My parents, fearing that they would lose me and not see me again, refused the offer. I have always regarded this as a lost opportunity.

My father could neither speak nor write English. He told me later that he never had any opportunity to go to school during the early days of the colonial era when Rhodesia was still administered by the British South Africa Company of Cecil John Rhodes. He had, however, taught himself to read and write in Ndebele. My mother, too, had not gone to school. Consequently, we, the children could not speak English. Our language at home was Ndebele. Because of our association with the Africans we learnt to speak *Karanga*, the local Shona dialect. Shabani (now called Zvishavane) is in the Midlands Province where the spoken languages are *Karanga* and Ndebele. Because the Mine employed a lot of foreign workers from Malawi (or Nyasaland as it was then called) there was a large community of Nyanja speaking people in Shabani. Consequently, I became very fluent in *Ndebele, Karanga* and *Nyanja*.

Karanga is a *Shona* dialect spoken in the region of *Masvingo* which is quite distinct from that spoken in Mashonaland.

Life was very tough for us. We tried to mingle, make friends, play and interact with our African neighbours most of whom spoke the *Shona* or *Karanga* language. I always felt somewhat insecure as many would give me a hostile look or stare at me as if I had just dropped from outer space. At times some would hurl insults at me and call me derogatory names such as "*Nkau*" meaning an albino or "*Murungu dondo*" meaning a lost white person/bush white man. I also used to receive insults from the Ndebeles, albeit less frequently, who would occasionally call me "*Igola*" meaning a wild cat, on account of the green pigmentation of my eyes' iris.

Because, from time to time, I would be challenged with such racial slurs I became somewhat aggressive and defiant and always ready to attack or to defend myself. I can recall several incidents early in my life when I would be confronted by such hostility just because I was light-skinned. One day as I was passing a house in the compound, not very far from our house, a young boy about my age said to me "*Murungu dondo*". Without any hesitation I chased after him and he darted and dashed into his family home. I followed him into his parent's home and gave him a thrashing in his own house right before his mother and other members of his family. Such incidents, although rare, would happen from time to time.

Our house did not have any water reticulation system. There was no running water in the house. Water had to be collected in cans or drums from a communal water source nearby for domestic use. For bathing our family had to use a portable zinc bath tub. The tub would be filled with cold water and then we would be bathed. In winter, water was heated in a drum or a bucket on a wood fire and then poured into the bath tub. We had a wooden stove for cooking our meals. The floors in the house were all made of cement. The house had an asbestos roof and there was no ceiling.

Because we all loathed using the public latrine, we used to go into the nearby bush and squat to use the toilet. Fortunately, our house was the last house bordering the bush.

One incident remains etched on my mind. On this particular day I was enjoying myself playing a game with friends when my mother decided it was time for me to take a bath. I explained to my mother and my two sisters,

Kathleen and Ava, that I was not quite ready to take a bath. I was in the middle of a game with some friends and I did not want to stop and take a bath. This did not go well with my mother who, with the help of the two girls, forced me, kicking and screaming, to take a bath. I was so angry that, as soon as they had finished bathing me, I jumped out of the bath and rolled on the sand as a protest to their actions. Undaunted, they grabbed me, once again, and put me into the bath. Realizing that I was fighting a losing battle I decided to change my tactics. I picked up some stones and started to pelt them. They all ran and took refuge in the house and barricaded themselves. They remained under siege until my father returned from work at which time I hid the stones and pretended that nothing had happened. I was punished but then let into the house when it got dark outside.

Such was my character in those early days. My militancy got me into a lot of trouble to the extent that my parents were worried as to what sort of person I would eventually turn out to be. Looking back now I believe that my attitude was caused by the fact that I did not like the situation I found myself in, i.e. being Coloured. I didn't like being treated any differently from the whites or blacks around me. I loathed being Coloured. I did not even want to be called Coloured or addressed as such by anybody. I just wanted to be me – no classification. My belligerence persisted until I reached adulthood.

Sometime in late 1949 or early 1950 my mother was taken ill. I have not been able to ascertain the real cause of the illness. In hindsight; I suspect that she may have contracted asbestosis from asbestos exposure from the mine dumps. My father decided to send her back to her home village at Bokodo in Filabusi. Kathleen, Ava and I accompanied her, but Stephen went to live on *Sifuka's* farm in *Shamba* to, I was later told, look after my father's cattle. This arrangement was a precursor to the release of the cattle which, ostensibly, belonged to my father but held by Sifuka. Steven was to look after the cattle for a period of one year after which the cattle would be released. Sifuka had said that he needed to be compensated for all the time that he had taken to look after the cattle. This arrangement has never made any sense to me but, it seems, my father agreed to it. Perhaps he did this out of desperation.

My mother remained in Bokodo for some time. Her condition deteriorated, and she died. I was four years old at the time and I did not understand the significance of death. I remember when asking my uncle *Kesari* why there were so many people about and who was being buried. He lied to me saying that the people had gathered to bury a chicken. In my heart I knew that my mother had died and that this was her burial. Not long after this I was told that Steven had also died, possibly poisoned by *Sifuka*.

My maternal grandmother, who briefly looked after Ava and I after my mother had passed away, was very kind to us. However, her husband *uNkinki*, my step-grandfather, did not like us at all always indicating to my grandmother and the other members of his family that he did not wish to look after *amagola* or wild cats. I believe that his hatred for us stemmed from the fact that we were not his biological off-springs and Ava and I being light skinned or Coloured brought shame to him. My biological maternal grandfather, *umKhamo*, had died some years before. *UNkinki*, as the eldest younger brother had married my grandmother in accordance with the Ndebele custom.

When I returned to Shabani in early 1951 after the death of my mother, I was surprised to find a strange woman at home in Shabani. I was told that she was my new mother. Her name was *uMadhlodhlo*. She made it obvious from the start that she didn't like me. This was the beginning of a very difficult phase of my life.

uMadhlodhlo was a widow past child bearing age. She had two adult children, a boy and a girl, who were grown-up and had their own homes. They would come to visit us from time to time. The boy's name was *umVinjelwa Matshazi* and the girl was Esther *Hlabangana*.

My sisters were no longer living with us. Kathleen remained with my grandmother *uMazondo* in Bokodo but was never sent to school. Ava came briefly to Shabani but was taken away to be a baby sitter for my aunt Rhoda at *eLangeni* in Belingwe (now Mberengwa). I remained under the sole care of my step-mother, *uMadhlodhlo* because most of the time my father would be at work or would travel away to visit friends and relatives in Malole, Gwatemba.

There are times when my father would be away from home. While he was away *uMadhlodhlo* would visit her friends and, perhaps have something to eat there, and not cook at home. In such instances I would sleep hungry without any food whatsoever.

uMadhlodhlo had her ancestral home near *Vukwe,* in the *Mazwiwa Tribal Trust lands*, which was 12 miles from Shabani. Often, when my father was away, she would decide to pay a visit to her home. Because she had nowhere to leave me she was obliged to take me with her. I always dreaded these trips for I found the distance to be very far for me to walk and exhausting. We would rise early in the morning to start on our journey. She was a thin strong woman and could walk very fast without stopping anywhere on the way to take a rest. I always had to run behind her in order to keep up for I was only about 5 years old and my legs were short and my steps small. I was always fearful of being left behind as I was certain, in my childish mind, that there were all manner of beasts lurking behind the tall grass and bushes flanking the roadside. By the time we arrived at the village I would be so tired that I would fall asleep almost instantly until next morning and by then it would be time to make the return journey home.

At the beginning of 1952 we had an unexpected visit from my aunt *uNkungulu*, my late mother's younger sister, accompanied by an escort. She had been sent as an envoy by the Dhlamini family to demand the lobola or bride price for my late mother. The conditions were that, if my father was not able to deliver 10 head of cattle or the equivalent thereof in money, Ava and I would be taken to live with her as bond for payment of the lobola. **In reality we were being taken into slavery**, but I did not know it or realize this at the time.

My father had not been able to raise the money for the lobola when he had married my mother some 14 years previously. Even after getting a job and working for the Mine he was still not able to afford the lobola. The only way he could ever raise the money was through taking possession of his cows that were still held by Sifuka. Despite numerous attempts, he had not been able to get his cattle from Sifuka who had acquired the cattle from my grandfather as trustee for my father and his three sisters. Relentless efforts to collect the cattle had proved fruitless. My aunt Gem told me many years later that she believed that my brother Steven had been poisoned by Sifuka to discourage my father from making any further claims for his cattle.

As my father was in no position to raise the lobola I was forced to go and live with my aunt and her husband at *koSingoma* (in Ndebele) or *kwaChingoma* (in Karanga). We travelled by Shu-Shine Bus Service, passed Belingwe, Mnene, *Mataga* Growth Point and arrived at *Musume* Mission where we came off the bus and were taken by a pick-up truck to Christopher *Ncube's* home. Christopher was married to my aunt *Nkungulu*. Neighbours referred to this village as "*komBishop*" i.e. home of the Bishop.

The residence had a two-bedroom house, surrounded by several pole and *dagga* huts two of which served as bedrooms and third was used as a kitchen. There was also a large granary at the rear of the house. Adjacent to the house and outside the perimeter of the residence, there were several pole and dagga huts occupied by families of people seeking healing from various ailments. Some were crippled, and some possessed by demons or just having what was said to be incurable diseases. Many had come because he was a self-appointed prophet and a renowned spiritual healer. He also claimed to prophesy and able to foretell the future. I was told that he often performed miraculous healing, although throughout my five year stay there I did not witness any.

He was revered and addressed as a Bishop (or *umBishop*) and had many cultic followers. He had an impressive organizational structure with his top lieutenants being designated as president (or *uMongameli*), elders and deacons. These people were zealous worshippers of God who strictly kept Saturday as the Sabbath. They were, in many ways similar to the Jews in their strict observance of the Sabbath day rest. Every Friday at sunset all work, including the cooking of meals, ceased until sunset on Saturday. A worship service was conducted at which a sermon was preached every Sabbath (i.e. Saturday) and was attended by members from the surrounding communities including some from the vaRemba community. In his absence, an elder or deacon would lead the service and the lingua franca was *Ndebele*.

In some ways he was treated as if he was supernatural. This can be illustrated by the fact that, whenever you were about to enter or exit a room in which he was seated or sleeping, you were required to kneel and seek his permission.

It did not matter how many times you entered or left the room, you were required to seek his permission otherwise you would be in breach of protocol. At first, I found this practice to be rather silly and ridiculous but after a while I became accustomed to it and it became quite natural and normal.

UmBishop, as he was popularly known, had about twenty acres of land under rain fed farming system. Regularly planted on this land were such crops, as maize, millet, sorghum, *nyimo* bean, peanut or groundnut, pumpkin, *amakhomane* or squash, water melon, potatoes and sweet potatoes. He had no tractors or motorized farm equipment relying mainly on oxen drawn ploughs and harrows to cultivate the soil in preparation for sowing seed or planting to loosen or turn the soil, as well as to harrow the fields, to kill or remove weeds.

Followers of this church came from a wide area of the Midlands and Matabeleland South Province stretching all the way to Mwenezi District. Members were expected to pay or return a tithe and a free will offering. As a result, umBishop and his wife had a pretty comfortable lifestyle.

Clifford, my cousin and my aunt's first born son was a year younger than I was. He had siblings whose names where *Latti*, *Tamatisi* (meaning a tomato), *Florence* and *Beauti*. Later on, two more children were born, and they were *Macloud* and *Bigboy*.

As a 6-year-old boy I found life at koSingoma very challenging to say the least. My regular chores included looking after cattle, milking cows etc. During the summer months I had added duties of leading oxen as they ploughed or harrowed the crop fields. In winter I had to load cattle manure from the cow pens onto a mule drawn Scotch cart or wooden sleigh, take it to the fields and empty it into heaps getting it ready for spreading on the lands when the ploughing season began. I would, also take part in chopping firewood and stacking it in bundles ready for use. Clifford did not perform the same chores as I did. His job was to look after a few donkeys around the premises. It was not uncommon for me to be awakened very early in the morning at around 4:00 a.m., during the ploughing season, to lead oxen ploughing or harrowing the fields whilst Clifford was asleep.

On one occasion in 1952 my father sent me a pair of khaki shorts and trousers. My aunt took the clothes, gave the trousers to Clifford and then handed me the shirt. As I did not have any other clothes at that time to wear I had to walk around only wearing the shirt. This was very embarrassing as I was six years old. Fortunately, the shirt was very long. However, not very long after this, my father sent some more clothes which were given only to me when my uncle *Kesari* intervened.

Sometimes I was tasked with assisting my uncle *Kesari* who, by this time, had come to live with us following the *Bokodo* community's forced relocation to *Jotsholo*, to load 50kg bags of maize on donkeys or mules and take the grain to a mill in *Musume*, about 10 miles away, to be ground, and then return with the mealie meal. *Sadza*, a hard porridge made from mealie meal (or maize meal), was our staple food. Other times I was tasked with taking the cattle to the dip tank which was 15 miles away. Walking barefoot to the mill and to the dip tank was very tiring indeed.

Ava arrived at koSingoma in the summer of 1952 from eLangeni where she had gone to baby sit for my aunt Rhoda. She was immediately given domestic chores to perform such as cooking, washing, going to the well to fetch and bring water to the house. In summer there were also other duties like sowing seeds, spreading manure on the lands, planting, weeding, making fire, harvesting the crops by hand as there was no harvesting equipment, etc. We were kept so busy that we hardly met or talked with one another.

I had many stressful experiences whilst herding cattle. At one time I came across a congress of baboons numbering at least thirty. Baboons have been known to be the loudest, most obnoxious, most viciously aggressive and least intelligent of all primates. I had not seen a baboon before. The baboons, sensing that I was young and afraid of them, would come towards me and make loud barks to frighten me. I was terrified but relieved when they eventually decided to leave and go their way.

My main occupation since arriving at koSingoma was herding cattle. I would get up early every morning, except on Saturdays, open the cattle kraal to let out the cattle and drive them to pasture. Pastures were far and beyond and behind the mountains overlooking the village. I had to drive the cattle through a mountain pass to a valley beyond. It was here that I spent five years of my life.

Looking after cattle was pretty boring to say the least. Whilst the cattle grazed I found myself searching the bush for wild berries. As breakfast was never provided I had to live by my wits. As time went by I became adept at identifying wild fruits. My knowledge of the bush and its fruits became very useful to me in later years when I was in the Rhodesian Army.

The koSingoma area of Mberengwa was rich in wild berries. The following are some of the berries that I came to know and pick as a herdsman: *Umkhemeswane, Umbumbulu, Ikhiwane, Umganu, Umklampunzi, UmKhomo, Umviyo, Intakubomvu, Ilihlolenkomo, Uxakuxaku, Umthunduluka, Ihabahava, Isadenda, Umtshwankela, Idolofia, Umwawa, Isigangatsha, Ububese, Umdlawuzo, Umqokolo,*

Ubhunzu, Umkhuna, Ikhabe lenyoka, Utshwala benyoni, Idololenkonyane and Umnyi. Needless to say, I was never hungry.

Sometimes I would be pre-occupied with gathering these berries that I would not immediately notice that the cattle had moved to other pastures. It was from such instances that I learnt how to track by following the spoor and observing the disturbances to the grass and soil and studying the freshness of the dung.

I met and became friends with the vaRemba herdsmen. The *Lemba* (vaRemba in Shona and *avaLemba* in Ndebele) have existed as small groups all the way from Nyanga plateau to the *Soutpansberg* in South Africa. They claimed to be descendants of Muslim Arabs on the East Coast. During Mfecane, some of the *VaRemba* in Mberengwa fled to the Venda area of South Africa. When the security situation improved, some of them trekked back to settle in Mberengwa, where they are still to be found under Chief *Mposi*, who was a tributary chief under the Ndebeles. To this day some of the vaRemba adhere to cultural practices that point to an Arab origin. Circumcision is just one example.

The *vaRemba* were excellent at spear fishing. I would spend most times learning how to catch fish using a spear. They performed this feat without diving underwater. The secret of success, they taught me, was to aim lower below the fish as the clear water created an optical illusion. Although I put a lot of effort into it I just could not master the art. We used always to search for calm and shallow waters as we preferred such waters for spearing fish from above the surface, as water clarity was of utmost importance.

One day while I was fishing with my *vaRemba* friends I came across a beautiful shiny black stone. It was different from all the stones I had seen before. I took it home. Christopher, my aunt's husband saw it in my hand and asked me where I had found it. I told him where I had found it and later took him to the place where there was an abundance of them. Later that year or the following year there was a lot of activity with huge trucks passing our village laden with equipment. I later discovered that Christopher had taken the chrome sample to a mining prospector who had paid him £500 and staked a claim to establish a chrome mine. I was disappointed that he did not thank me or acknowledge that it was because of my discovery that he had such good fortune. Christopher had bought himself a beautiful pick-up truck and all along I had been wondering how he could afford it.

Such was my life as a herdsman at koSingoma tribal land. Very often we would be preoccupied with spear fishing or some other activity that I would lose the cattle and later find them in a maize field eating the neighbours' crops. Sometimes I would find the cattle before the owners discovered them and I would drive them out hurriedly to conceal the fact and avoid punishment. Sometimes I would find them when it was too late. In such instances I would just leave them, stay out of sight, look for a cave to shelter in, and not go home hoping that by the time they come searching for me and finding me they would have cooled down.

On one such occasion whilst I was in hiding I came across a klipspringer (*Igogo* in *Ndebele*) and it started to run. I chased it and by some stroke of good luck its horns were caught and entangled in the nearby bushes making it easy for me to kill it. I cut its throat to allow as much blood as possible to flow out.

My situation had suddenly changed. No longer was I that timid boy obsessed with the fear of being whipped. I enjoyed the prospect of being hailed a hero. I started to imagine myself a real hunter.

Carrying the carcass home presented me with a bit of a challenge as the animal weighed between 10 to 18 kilograms and the village was at least 5 miles away. I placed the animal on my shoulders and started to walk stopping now and again to rest and change shoulders until I arrived home when it was getting dark.

Meat in any form was considered a luxury and only eaten on rare occasion such as at Christmas or during weddings or other celebrations. Our staple diet was *Isitshwala* (in *IsiNdebele*), or Sadza (in Shona) accompanied with *umbida* (in *IsiNdebele*), *Muriwo* (in *Shona*) or *Murivo* (in *Karanga*). Sometimes it would be accompanied with beans or *amas*i (sour milk). Most people looked forward to sadza with a meat stew. When I arrived home with a klipspringer on my back every one was very excited. No wonder I was given a hero's welcome. No mention was made about me letting the cattle into a neighbour's field.

Kathleen was left in Bokodo. She was never sent to school. I never heard from her for some years until the time she visited me to help me escape from koSingoma. I always regarded her visit as a godsend. This visit always reminds me of the story in the Bible when Moses turned up in Egypt after 40 years to rescue the Israelites from the bondage of Pharaoh. My situation, I often thought, was similar to that of the Israelites who were in bondage to the Egyptians for 430 years.

In January 1953 I was kitted out to begin school at *Gwavamtangwi* School. The school was about 5 or 6 miles away. As we had to walk this distance this meant that we had to rise very early in the morning in order to make it to school on time. We would prepare our packed lunch, usually consisting of stamped mealies or boiled beans depending on the season. We would carry our food in a small container and cover it with a lid.

The school had no facilities at all apart from the classrooms with desks and some slates to write on. There was no canteen or an ordinary room where the children could store their belongings. We were expected to bring our food in the morning from home. This meant that, before entering the class you had to find a place to hide the food. Sometimes you would find a suitable spot under or next to a shrub. Other times you would need to dig a hole and bury your food container. It was always a good idea to mark the spot so you do not forget it when time came to eat the food. There was always the risk that someone would see you hiding the food and steal it before you could retrieve it.

All the children in the school were African except for me and my sister, Ava. With our light skin complexion, we stuck out like a sore thumb. There were always curious gazes from all around us as though we had just dropped out of the sky. At interval time we would hear some derogatory comments or racial slurs. I could never understand why some people would display so much insensitivity. Perhaps that is how the world is, I thought. Only the children who came from the villages near to ours and had come to know us were friendly towards us.

I was seven years old when I started school. I was placed in Sub A which is the equivalent of kindergarten or year 1 today. All the children in my class were much older than I was. Our Class Teacher's name was Johnson and we were told to address him as Teacher Johnson.

Gwavamtangwi School was very primitive with inadequate teaching resources. We were given slates to write on. There were very few textbooks and we relied mostly on reading what had been written, by the teacher, on a chalk blackboard.

It was not long before I grasped the concepts of Arithmetic and the English language. The teacher was very impressed with my ability and it was not long before he appointed me as his assistant to help the other pupils to grasp the concepts. Because of this, many of my classmates, especially those who just could not understand what was going on, resented me and sometimes mocked me. However, there were some who were pleased with the help that I could give and we became friends.

The following year, instead of going to Sub B, I was promoted to Standard One. Even in this class, my school performance was above average. I received numerous awards for Spelling and Arithmetic. I was also at the top of my class at every examination.

Ava was enrolled in a higher class than I as this was not her first year in school. She, too, was experiencing a backlash from those of her age group. She did not like or enjoy what had befallen us. From the outset, she started to do the groundwork and planned for our escape back to Shabani to be reunited with our father. However, it would be a long while and after several attempts before this could happen.

We became involved in many of the school's activities. I was inducted into the school choir. Because of my light skin colour among the sea of black faces I did all I could to get out of the choir as I did not feel at all comfortable taking part in choir-dance competitions that would take me to other schools. There were other activities that I got involved in such as agriculture and gardening. I did not enjoy these activities either. I found them to be back-breaking work as the school did not have water hoses or irrigation systems. This meant we would spend much of our time carrying heavy buckets of water, to and fro, to water plants and vegetables.

Returning home from school we would find our chores waiting for us. It was tiring work. By the end of the day I could hardly keep my eyes open whilst waiting to have supper. After supper there was another period of waiting for worship. Invariably I would fall asleep and the deacon in charge would rudely awaken me by pouring cold water on my face. I often thought to myself, "What kind of Christianity is this?"

I used to look forward to Friday evenings and Saturdays. Friday evening was the beginning of the Sabbath. All work ceased before sunset. That meant that all livestock would be rounded up and into the pens or kraals long before sun-set followed by a worship service after which I was free to go to sleep. Saturday was the day of worship during which we worshiped God in a relaxed atmosphere. Work began after sun-set on Saturday after which I would start to have a lot of foreboding.

One afternoon I was told that I needed to be baptized along with other people in the village, including my cousin Clifford. The next Sabbath we were given white robes and ushered to the nearby "Jordan" river. The whole congregation gathered along the bank of the river and, after much singing of the hymns, we were immersed into the water. As we came out of the water, the Bishop breathed on each of us and pronounced his blessing.

Whenever I had an opportunity to meet with Ava, we would talk about our predicament. She would update me on our escape plan. I looked forward to these meetings with much anticipation.

In about the beginning of 1954 we noticed a hive of activity taking place by a nearby river. Curious to find out what was happening Ava and I drew near and saw a white man surrounded by a group of black men. There was a lot of earth-moving equipment about. He introduced himself as James Goodall, the dam builder, and asked us where we were from and we told him.

He went to his caravan and brought us some sweets and chocolates and we thanked him and left. As we went on our way I could remember the look on his face and thought to myself that he liked Ava, but I did not say anything to her about it. Not long after he began to make frequent visits to our village and telling Ava that he would take us away after completing his dam project. My aunt *Nkungulu* and her husband were either oblivious of his designs or may have thought he was not serious about taking Ava away with him. They continued to accept his gifts which included such provisions as tea, sugar, jams, bread, etc. for as long as he offered them.

The relationship went on for a long time and *Nkungulu* and umBishop continued to accept his gifts. Time came when construction of the dam came to an end, and he announced to them that he was coming, on a certain day, to collect Ava and me and take us away.

There was a great deal of panic and they decided to hide Ava from Mr. Goodall. She was taken to a village about half a mile away. They told Mr. Goodall that Ava had returned to her father in Shabani. I was present when he came to demand for Ava. It did not occur to them that my presence would arouse suspicion in Mr. Goodall's mind.

Mr. Goodall came over to the village compound intending to take Ava away. When informed she was not around he became irate and threatened to destroy the huts with his truck. He suspected that she had been hidden because I was still around. Everyone left the village and hid in the bushes nearby until evening. Eventually he gave up and left the village. Ava remained hidden for some time until they became satisfied that he had left koSingoma altogether.

In November 1954 Ava decided it was time for us to leave and return to Shabani. It had been raining for some time and the ground was very wet. We decided to walk through the bush veldt, cross the *Mundi* River to *Musume* Growth Point and take a bus from there to Shabani the next morning. We had saved some money for the fares.

Ava was fifteen and I was eight years old. We started our journey at dawn. It was pouring with heavy rain. We did not suspect that the river may be in flood. We covered the 8-mile journey rather quickly and reached our crossing point.

We arrived at the southern bank of the *Mundi* River and hesitated. We had never seen this river at this level of flooding before. I was afraid. Undaunted, Ava asked me to jump on her back, which I did, and she started walking forward into the water. As we moved forward I noticed there were, logs, branches and other debris floating downstream past us on either side. Ava waded forward until the water level reached her waist. Suddenly, Ava dropped into an unseen hole causing the water level to go up to her shoulders and causing my upper body, limbs and feet to be suspended and floating horizontally. With my feet dangling, I tightened my grip around Ava's neck in fear of being swept away. Ava had fallen into a rock pool and we could neither go forward nor back. We were stuck and panic set in.

At that very moment we saw a man across the river. He shouted at us to stand still as he waded towards us. At the same time, we heard our uncle *Kesari's* voice behind as he walked into the river to rescue us. I was relieved but disappointed that the rescue came from our uncle rather than from the man that was across the river.

Arriving back at the village life went back to normal once again as we resumed our usual daily routine. We tried as best we could to forget about us ever getting out of this hell hole. We often wondered how long we could tolerate living in such conditions of total slavery. Ava did not give up but always cherished the hope of leaving the place to go back to Shabani.

All the grades at *Gwavamtangwi* School went up to Standard 3 and it was not long before Ava had to leave the school. She was enrolled as a boarder at *Musume* Mission which had been established by the Church of Sweden Mission (CSM) in 1932. Ava attended this school for one single term and was back at home with no school to go to. She later told me that she was not being taught anything. The sister in charge was using her as her nanny and she left.

In July or August 1956 Ava was still at home and no arrangement had been made for her to attend school. One afternoon, Ava, *Nkungulu*, I and several other people were under an *Msasa* tree plucking peanuts that had just been harvested. An argument erupted between Ava and *Nkungulu*. Suddenly Ava threw down the bunch of nuts she had been plucking, got up and walked away. She crossed the fence which was some 200 yards away and disappeared into the nearby bush.

My first thought about the incident was that, after her anger had cooled, she would return. At nightfall we stopped work and went home, expecting to find Ava at home. It soon became evident that she had left. Efforts to find her proved fruitless. I began to suspect that she had run away. I was disappointed that she had left without me.

At Christmas time in December 1957 both my sisters, Kathleen and Ava, who were now living in Shabani, paid us a visit. I was thrilled for I had not seen Kathleen since I was about three or four years old. I had not also seen Ava since her sudden departure nearly eighteen months ago. They brought me clothes, sweets and chocolates. We had a wonderful Christmas together.

As the time for their departure drew nigh, they told me that they had come to fetch me and that I should prepare to leave. They also informed me that there would be a pick-up truck vehicle that would take us to *Musume* Growth Point. We arranged that on the day of their departure I would say goodbye to them and leave the village unnoticed, walk through the bush and wait for them at a predetermined rendezvous point on the road to *Musume* Growth Point. I was exhilarated. Freedom had come at last I thought. I did as I was instructed.

Full of hope and excitement I waited eagerly for them to come and soon enough the pick-up arrived, and I jumped at the back of the truck and we travelled to *Musume* Growth Point. On arrival at *Musume* we checked in at the local motel for the night.

Next morning the bus arrived, and we boarded. Unknown to us, umBishop had risen early that morning to intercept us with the hope of taking me back to the village with him. Before the bus could leave there was serious confrontation between Kathleen and umBishop in the presence of a bus load of passengers. His demand for me to be released to him was resisted by both my sisters with the help of the bus driver and passengers. Eventually he gave up and left.

CHAPTER 9

Life in Shabani

WE TRAVELLED SAFELY to Shabani. My father and his wife, *uMadhlodhlo*, were no longer living at Nil Mine Village where I had left them. They had moved out and had established a new residence in a neighbourhood called *koMpapusi*, in keeping with his desire to live in a secluded environment. My father was one of many Coloured people who had approached a Mr. *Papenfus* to rent a piece of land on his farm. My grandmother, *uMsoli*, whom I had not met before, had come to live with us following the death of her husband.

They built a beautiful house on a *kopje* overlooking the *Maglas* Village. It had 2 bedrooms, a dining room and 2 adjacent pole and dagga huts, one of which served as a kitchen. The other hut was used as a bedroom which I shared with my grandmother.

Conversing in *Ndebele* with my grandmother, whom I addressed as "*ugogo*" I got to learn a little bit about my grandfather, Pat. She used to talk a lot about him and how she met him as a young virgin and how she had been given to him by her father, *uMajinkila*, as a bride. Whenever she wanted to reminisce about her early life, she would refer to him as Pat. She never forgot the taste of butter that Pat used to make on the farm.

Often, my grandmother would refer to my grandfather as Holl (or *uHollo* as she would speak it). I always assumed she was meaning Hall as, on my birth certificate, we had been registered as Hall. It was not until many years later that I discovered that we should have been registered as Holl as our grandfather's name was Harry Patrick Holl. The error arose because my father had not known how to spell his father's name.

uMsoli often lamented the fact that she had turned down Pat's offer to build her a house on his farm where she could have remained with her children after he had ended the marital union to marry a white woman. She would end our conversation by saying, "maybe *Hitler* would have received an education and not suffer as he has done." *Hitler* was a nickname given to my father because of his temperament.

My grandmother would often tell me stories about her father, *Majinkila*. She would also relate stories of how her grandfather, *Mhabahaba*, had run away from Tshaka, with Mzilikazi to settle in koBulawayo and how he was banished to live *in eMbelengwa* amongst the *vaRemba* tribe.

My grandmother was an extremely clean and hygienic person. Despite her age she insisted that our room be kept spotlessly clean. She would not go to bed without bathing. She was also a very religious person and a staunch Seventh Day Adventist just like my father. We prayed together every night and every morning, and, on every Sabbath, she would get me to escort her to church for services.

My step-mother, *uMadhlodhlo* was not at all enthusiastic about my return. She refused to let me move into the spare bedroom in the main house. She insisted that the room had been reserved for visitors.

When I first visited Shabani Town Centre I was shocked how racist the white people were. There were some places that were reserved for whites, such as the main hotel situated in the middle of the town. You could not just enter any restaurant to eat.

In January 1958 I enrolled at Jeffrey Hooper School for Coloured children. At that time, it was the only school that I could attend in Shabani. There were other schools but, they were reserved for white children or African children. This was due to the settler colonial administration's policy of separate development existing at that time.

Our school was situated on a hill overlooking the town. The school was under resourced. There was no library and there were only two teachers – Mrs. Fisher and Mr. Naidoo. Mr. Naidoo doubled up as both teacher and headmaster. All the Children, from Sub A to Standard 5 were housed in 2 classrooms Mrs. Fisher teaching the younger grades and Mr. Naidoo the older grades. Mr. Naidoo was from India or Ceylon (Sri Lanka as it is now known). Mrs. Fisher was Coloured from Belingwe.

It was a very small school when I first got there. We were few in number such that it was not feasible to field a soccer team. The sport we could play was Rounders, an old English game that never became a seriously competitive sport, although it is probably an ancestor of Baseball. This game could be played with relatively few children.

The school was later relocated to Eastleigh, a Coloured suburb about 3 miles from town. However, by the time it was moved, I had left the school.
I attended this school until I completed Standard 5 at the end of 1960. Both my sisters were married by now.

Late in 1958, my father received a notice, from Mr. *Papenfus*, to vacate the land on which we were living. Sadly, my father had to tear down his lovely house and the two huts. *uMadhlodhlo* took all the materials to her home in Vukwe. We had no choice but to go and live at *Maglas* Village, very much against the wishes of my father and me. We later moved back to Nil Mine.

Salaries paid to non-white employees of the Mine were significantly low compared to those paid to whites. However, the mine did provide weekly dry rations which included bread, rice, cassava, mealie meal, dried beans and dried salt fish known as *bakayawo*. Such provisions went a long way to sustain the lives of the black families, including our own. I recall, on several occasions, having to join the queue to collect my father's rations from the Mine's Welfare Department.

By this time my grandmother, *uMsoli*, had been taken to go and live with her daughter, Gem in Gokwe where she later died in 1970. She had refused to go and live with us in the Location, as the African housing was called.

Growing up as a young boy in Shabani, I often thought of how I was suffering pernicious discrimination and xenophobia just because I was born Coloured. However, as I was growing up I came to realize that Rhodesia was not the only country in the world to have such endemic discrimination. At about this time I started to read newspapers and hear about Martin Luther King's civil rights movement. The problem was that the blacks also discriminated against me. Was it because my skin colour closely resembled that of a white man?

The general atmosphere at this school was a lot better than that of *Gwavamtangwi* School. There were no longer any racial insults hurled at me to contend with as the rest of the school children were also Coloured. The school was, however, divided into two groups; those that lived in the suburb and those that lived in the surrounding African villages or locations. In general, those children who came from the Coloured suburb tended to shun those that lived in the locations.

When I first arrived at the school we were living in our home on Mr. *Papenfus'* Farm in a small Coloured community; so, the stigma of poverty was not easily discernible. However, when all the Coloureds were evicted and we had to go and live at *Maglas* Village I tried to conceal this fact from my friends. I remember one incident when a school friend's parent offered me a lift home I opted to be dropped at a point in town and walked all the way in the rain. I did this because I was ashamed of being poor. However, I could not keep the pretense for long. On another day, after I had joined the Scout Movement, after a session the Scout Master offered me a lift home along with other boys. It was late in the evening; so, I had no choice but to accept. From that day on all the children knew that I lived in the African location and would tease me about this.

There was another problem that I faced. I shared a surname of "Hall" with a wealthy Coloured family. They owned a fleet of buses and trucks and had a palatial home by Shabani's Standards. Wherever I went in Shabani and, later on, anywhere in Rhodesia I would be asked if I was related to the "Halls". Each time I had to say, "No". This was annoying to me so much that when I discovered that my family name was "Holl" I immediately changed it to "Holl" by deed poll.

In general, school life in Shabani was a lot better than I had experienced in Belingwe. I had a very close friend by the name of Joseph. He was smart and was always thinking of ingenious ways to raise money so that we would always have pocket money to spend. We received most of our income from caddying at the local Golf Club. Most of the school children would spend their pocket money on fish and chips at the restaurant adjacent to the school run by a Greek couple whom we nicknamed Mr. and Mrs. *Nyonyo*. Because we were such regular customers Mrs. *Nyonyo* would put aside crumbs or "*mafufu*" (which is Ndebele for crumbs) for us to eat during lean times when we had no money. Many of my friends would wonder how I would have money or be able to eat at *Nyonyo's* all year round.

It was around this time that my father received a visit from his youngest sister, Ruth. She brought her youngest son, Churchill, to attend school with me at Jeffrey Hooper School. I had been experiencing a lot of bullying from the Black boys in the location. With Churchill by my side the bullying stopped as we would respond with force against any unprovoked attacks or slur.

When the school closed in December 1960, I had no idea which school I was going to attend. The local secondary schools would not consider my application because I was Coloured. It looked like my school career had abruptly come to an end. The white schools would not accept me because I was not white, and the black schools would not enroll me because I was not black in terms of the government's classification.

Kathleen had left her husband, John, and had met and fallen in love with Enos. Enos was a politician and a member of the newly formed National Democratic Party (NDP), a political party founded by Joshua Nkomo. On finding out that I was Kathleen's young brother; he took a liking to me. He had a travelling companion who, also, was a politician belonging to the same party. His name was Morton. They were in Shabani to conduct political meetings designed to woo the people of Shabani to support and join the party. During their brief stay in Shabani they would ask me to accompany them to the meetings and I did. It was at this time that I realised that Nkomo was serious in his quest to mobilize the African population to fight white minority rule.

CHAPTER 10

Boarding School

MRS. NAIDOO, a *Coloured* woman living in our neighbourhood of *koMpapusi* had two sons Amin and Essop. Amin was in Standard 5 with me and Essop was in Standard 4. Their mother had enrolled them both at Embakwe Coloured School in Plumtree. For reasons unknown to me, she had decided that she was not going to send Essop in 1961. This decision suited me perfectly because it meant I would get a chance to get an education by taking Essop's place.

She came by our house in early January 1961 and asked me if I would like to take Essop's place. I was very thrilled to get this opportunity. However, I still had a problem; how was I going to raise the school fees? The school fee was about £166.00 per term. Furthermore, additional funds would be needed to purchase school uniforms. My father was earning only about £25.00 per month which was woefully inadequate.

Mrs. Naidoo suggested that I should go to the Welfare Department and approach them for their assistance. Armed with my standard 5 school report I approached the Welfare Department. Mrs. Naidoo accompanied me and was very helpful in explaining my situation to the man at the Welfare.

I was given an annual grant of £498.00 to cover the fees, per annum, paid proportionally, directly to the school at the beginning of each term. This, then, enabled me to attend school at Embakwe Catholic Mission which was about 22 miles from Plumtree and in the Catholic Archdiocese of Bulawayo. In addition, I was given a uniform voucher redeemable at certain stores in Shabani. However, my father had to meet the cost of casual and other clothing, train and bus fare plus pocket money.

It was in December 1960 that, when I came home one afternoon, I found my step-mother, *uMadhlodhlo*, had packed her belongings ready to leave. I immediately sensed that something was wrong when she departed, without uttering a word, for her home in the village at *Vukwe*, with tears in her eyes. I later found out that there had been a quarrel and an altercation between her and my father. Apparently, my father had caught her or discovered that she had a lover. The marriage was over. I was glad to see her go.

With *uMadlodlo* gone, the task of looking after the household fell on me and Churchill. We soon learned how to cook meals, clean the house and do the laundry in a very short space of time. We were happy to carry out all the household chores and to be useful to my father. I was also tasked by my father to do the groceries and other purchases for the household. Being thrift by nature, I carried out these duties successfully to the extent that, over time, my father was able to open a savings account; something that had never happened before.

According to a legend that I have heard, Embakwe Mission was founded in 1902 by the spirit medium *Njemhlophe*, who gave up throwing the bones as a witchdoctor after he converted to Christianity. He came at the behest of Catholic missionaries who soon followed, a Jesuit priest on horseback and three dauntless nuns, fresh from England in an ox wagon loaded with provisions, including a hen, a cock and a cat.

Initially, they turned back because of a thunderstorm with forked lightning. On the second attempt, the wagon got bogged down in mud. So, the nuns, from the Belgian-based Sisters of *Notre Dame de Namur*, footslogged through the slush to their new home.

By the time that I arrived at Embakwe in 1961 it was well developed, with the main buildings constructed of unplastered red brick, contoured and ornate. However, the ablution blocks were still very primitive. Although we had running water and were able to take showers, there were no flush toilets. However, by the time I left school, modern toilets had been installed.

It would be wrong to imagine that because it was reserved for us, we were highly privileged. The privilege, undoubtedly fundamental and vitally important, was that payment of basic fees by government was guaranteed. African black children were denied this.

However, as an educational institution, Embakwe was the poorest and most under-resourced of all schools in the colony. It was without both a science block and a library. I believe that the lack of these facilities had a negative impact on us all as it meant that none of us could aspire to become doctors or scientists after leaving school, especially people like me who had a liking for science subjects.

It is pertinent to point out that two great African schools in the Plumtree area, *Empandeni* and *Tekwane*, were both better resourced and each had a science block and a library. In addition, the outside World would only grant scholarships to Blacks, not Coloureds, as we were classified as "White" for educational purposes. However, this "White classification" gave us no access to scholarships to South African universities. So, to put it bluntly, we were cheated.

All three schools however were "slums", when compared with nearby Plumtree High School, reputably one of the best schools in the history of the country, and therefore reserved for Whites. Most of the children in Embakwe were from poorer families. The school also served as a "reform school", to which problematical children were committed, on court order.

Despite being under resourced one could have still have gotten a fine education, especially in the Arts curriculum. The curriculum was British and bright students left on attainment of either Cambridge School Certificate (CSC) or the General Certificate of Education (GCE "O"). However, there was no "A" level; so, if you wanted to go to University you needed to be accepted at Founders High in Bulawayo or Morgan High in Salisbury (now Harare). There was also a provision for those who were less academic to attain a College of Preceptors (COP) qualification, after three years of secondary education, to enable them to leave school early in pursuit of a trade. I daresay that many of the students fell into this category as witnessed by the fact that many left to become welders, plumbers, platelayers, etc.

I still remember people like Mr. Brown, Mr. Bowers, Mr. Davies and our legendary Head Mistress, Sister Mare Nungent SND who played a significant role in our development.

The time came for Amin and me to leave Shabani and head for Embakwe where we were going to spend the next five years as boarders. My father accompanied me to the bus station to board the Shu-Shine bus to Bulawayo where we would catch the train to Plumtree. In Bulawayo we were met by

Mr. and Mrs. MacDonald who drove us to their house where we spent the night. Also living with the MacDonalds at that time was a young lady named Caroline, half-sister to Amin. I also discovered that Mrs. MacDonald was Amin's half-sister. Mr. MacDonald knew my father as they had met several times in *eNkankezi*.

The next morning, we boarded the train to Plumtree. On arrival at Plumtree Railway Station we were met by Sister Mare and Mr. Taylor. Sister Mare introduced herself as the Head Mistress of Embakwe Mission School. We soon discovered that Mr. Taylor was the truck driver for the school. The truck was used mainly to ferry goods, provisions and parcels from Plumtree and also to transport a few people to Plumtree to board a train in instances where it would be uneconomical to hire the *Landela* bus.

We were instructed to take our suitcases and any other belongings to the truck nearby and these were loaded on to the truck. Next to the truck was a hired bus from *Landela* Bus Service Company. We were told to get into the bus and find a seat. When we were all seated the driver took us to the school amid all our apprehension and foreboding. Not long after boarding the bus we arrived at the school amid shouts of "new comers" and "new comers have arrived ".

After disembarking from the bus, we were addressed by Mr. Brown. The girls were immediately taken to the girls' hostel whilst we remained with Brown who took us on a tour of the school complex, showing us the church, the refectory and other buildings and finally, the dormitories and our beds.

At about one o'clock we were marched to the Refectory where we were given lunch. Sister Brigid was in charge of the kitchen. We had to remain standing whilst grace was being said and after the meal we were taken back to the boys' hostel where we were introduced to the Head Boy, John, who was nicknamed "*Whabayi*" on account of his pale green eyes. We were also given a rundown of the rules of the hostel as well as the dos and don'ts. After this we were free to do whatever we liked for the remainder of the day.

Soon after, I linked up with John, nicknamed "*Hobo*" (*Ndebele* name for Mongoose) and Jimmy, nicknamed "Skunky". Jimmy sometimes used the name "*Strydom*" and I could never quite understand why. Perhaps these two chaps had decided that we needed to have dessert after the scrumptious meal that we just had. I didn't know where they were taking me. Suddenly Jimmy jumped the fence and was in the school's vegetable garden and started to pass a couple of watermelons to us. He then jumped out of the garden after which we feasted on the melons and left feeling smug and contented. Such was my introduction to Embakwe life.

My initial impression of Embakwe was that it was more like a military establishment. Life was harsh and unforgiving. Mr. Brown was more like a sergeant major than a teacher. He instilled much fear in us.

Mr. Brown was the boys Hostel Master or Dean for the boys as well as being my biology teacher. We nicknamed him *"Zhizhizhi"* and "Gorilla" or "Gori" for short because he was very strict and brooked no nonsense. Everyone at the Boys hostel feared *Zhizhizhi* and would behave themselves whenever he was around.

We looked forward to Friday's when he would make trips to Bulawayo. We would, again, become subdued whenever he returned on Sunday evening. If, for some reason, he did not return on Sunday evening we would, once again, be rejoicing until the day of his return. Our duties, which included making our beds, cleaning the dormitory, ablution bock, the grounds surrounding the dormitories, were performed with military precision under the supervision of prefects duly appointed by the Dean.

When I first arrived at Embakwe there were no flushing toilets. There was in existence a system of bucket toilets. Cleaning of the toilets, which involved a process of emptying the buckets in a designated pit and replacing them, was, reserved for those who, for one reason or the other, were under punishment. Consequently, I tried as much as I could to avoid falling into this category.

Unlike Jeffrey Hooper School, where school attendance was dominated by children of the wealthy, at Embakwe many of the children were from poor and working-class families. This made my new environment more conducive to learning as I was not looked down upon by my peers as was the case in Shabani.

The majority of the Coloured children were from Ndebele speaking backgrounds; so I had a lot of friends with whom I could share stories. I guess this may have been the reason why I fell into the company of John nicknamed *"Hobo"* and Jimmy nicknamed *"Skunky"* on my first day. Both these boys had a *Ndebele* background.

When the first day of school arrived Amin and I were put back to Standard V. We were told that our assessment had not quite reached the level of Form 1. There wasn't much that we could do about this but to resolve to prove ourselves. It seemed to me that we had been disadvantaged by the fact that Amin and I were the only ones coming from an outside school whereas the other children going into Form 1 had been at Embakwe from their earlier grades.

In Standard V there was a plump girl by the name of Yvonne. She liked me, and I also liked her. I therefore did not mind remaining in Standard V to be near her. In fact, I worked my way to be sharing a desk with her. We really had a great time together. She would often receive parcels from home and she would give me sweets, chocolate and various other goodies. I didn't receive any parcels at any time for the duration of my boarding at the school.

Our relationship went well for some time. I guess she wanted more from the relationship than just holding hands under the desk. I, on the other hand, was very timid and terrified of girls. So, when she suggested that we should meet one evening at the pig sty, which was a popular place for boys to secretly meet with girls, I froze. The very idea of kissing a girl was unthinkable and scary to me. I felt trapped and had no option but to agree to our meeting that evening. However, when the appointed time for our meeting came I just could not go through with it; so, I stayed away. I guess it was because of this incident that I acquired the nickname "Dead".

The next time that Yvonne came to class she was livid. She gave me a cold shoulder and quickly changed her seating place in class. I could feel her resentment towards me. I was no longer receiving any chocolates or sweets from her. This was the end to our relationship.

At the end of each year the headmistress, Sr. Marie SND would have the whole school assembled in the Beit Hall. The purpose was to honour those who topped their class at the year-end examinations. Each star pupil who had come first in class or achieved the highest marks in mathematics were asked to stand-up to be showered with praise and given a prize.

My Standard V class teacher was Mr. Brown. My class performance was very impressive. Eileen, I and another boy by the name of John were on top of the class. Eileen and John were from Botswana. Most of the time, the top position would rotate between Eileen and me with John coming third. It was hardly surprising, therefore, that before the year was over, Eileen, Myself and John were moved to Form 1.

In Form 2 Eileen and I posed a challenge to our new class mates. The jostling for the top position was now between Eileen, I and another John. This struggle for supremacy continued until 1965 when we all left school. Very often during the year I would receive awards for attaining the highest marks in Mathematics.

Embakwe catered for Coloured children of varying backgrounds and from all parts of Rhodesia as well as neighbouring countries such as Zambia and Botswana. There were some really amusing characters. I recall meeting the three brothers, Albert, Stephen and John from Botswana. John was nicknamed "Goldie".

Goldie seemed to love to keep my company. Maybe this was because he saw me as someone who was very gullible for he loved to tell stories depicting him as a hero. He was very delusional to the extent that his stories defied logic or common sense. It seemed to me that he was living in a fantasy world as he would tell us of how he was often involved in rescuing a damsel in distress single handed.

In all his stories the damsel in distress would invariably turn out to be one girl that he was fixated with whose name was Iana. He always ended his stories of chivalry being comforted by and in the arms of Iana.

He often claimed that he was a marksman and a good shot with a rifle to the extent that he was able to shoot a one shilling coin and split it into four tickeys. He would repeat his stories to anyone who cared to listen. Of course, none of us believed his stories but we dared not argue with him as we did not wish to become bad friends with him. We would try to avoid him as much as we could to avoid having to listen to his often-repeated stories.

One day, Mr. Taylor, the school's truck driver, whom we had nicknamed *"umHwaba"*, which translates to "a dried piece of meat" in the Ndebele language brought a pellet gun. He handed the gun to Goldie to shoot a target that he had set a few yards away. Goldie took aim at the target and missed. He turned around to a group of us who were watching with keen interest and nonchalantly said that the reason he had missed the target was because the barrel of the pellet gun was crooked which was not true of course.

At first, I just could not understand how somebody could tell a fake story without batting an eyelid as though he really believed the story himself.

Eventually I got used to Goldie's stories and accepted him for what he was.

When I returned home from Embakwe in December 1962 I was surprised to discover that my father had married another woman. Her name was Emma, from Mazwiwa Tribal Trust Land. We used to address her as "*umaMoyo.*"

Following the breakdown of his marriage to *uMadhlodhlo* my father had met and was about to marry another *Ndebele* woman by the name of Esther *Hlabangana*. Esther died in childbirth. She was very much younger than he was.

Ever since my Brother Steven's death my father seemed to be obsessed with the idea of fathering another boy child. It appeared that he would stop at nothing. He desperately wanted another son. In desperation he resorted to finding any woman who was willing to bear him a son irrespective of her suitability or her past history.

Emma had no ability to run a household. She was not thrifty and did not know how to plan or to budget her expenditure. She would often take money from the household, buy items like mangoes or tomatoes to sell and, at the end of the day come home with less money than she had invested in the project. Sad of all is that she would not realize that she wasn't making any money from her business ventures. As a result, money would run out before the next pay day making it necessary for my father to borrow money from friends to make ends meet

In September of that year Emma gave birth to my half-sister. Emma's profligacy continued unabated. My financial needs were now being neglected or ignored. Often there would be no money in the house to buy me clothes and shoes for school.

Emma had no idea of how to take care of her baby. The baby would often mess herself and would remain unchanged for long periods of time. My father would step in to feed, change and clean the child whilst she would be "bailed out" after a drinking orgy.

I returned to Embakwe for my third year of Secondary education or Form III. 1963 was a very difficult year for me. My shoes were worn, and my clothes were shabby. My shoes had holes underneath them. My father improvised and took discarded motor-car tyres, cut them into shape and replaced the soles. I was very embarrassed to wear them as they made me an object of scorn and derision amongst my peers. Despite these challenges I hung on until the end of the year in order to write my College of Preceptors (COP) examinations which I passed with flying colours – all distinctions.

Sometime during that year the school received notification from the Welfare Department that grant payments for school fees would cease to all students attending private schools of which Embakwe was one. Because of my dire financial situation, I was quite prepared to leave school and seek an apprenticeship. However, Sr. Mare, our Head Mistress was very impressed by my performance that she had written a reference letter to the Welfare asking them to fund my school fees for the next two years so I could finish my "O" levels, enroll at Founders High to complete "A" Levels.

She specifically instructed me to tell the Welfare department that my desire was to become a School Teacher and that I needed to complete GCE "A" Level and attend the Teachers' Training College in Hillside, Bulawayo. At that time the country had embarked on an ongoing and intensive recruitment campaign for Teachers and Nurses and she surmised that if I told the Welfare Department that I wanted to be a Teacher they would continue to fund my school fees.

Although I was somewhat reluctant, because of my financial situation, during the December break of that year, I took the letter from Sr. Mare, and handed it to the person in charge at the Welfare Department and told them that I needed to continue school for a further two-year period so that I could realize my ambition of becoming a Teacher.

My situation at home continued to deteriorate. Each holiday resulted in a family confrontation every time when the time came for me to go back to school. There would be an altercation between Emma and my father the night before I left to return to school. I began to lose my self-confidence. My grades began to deteriorate. I suddenly had a growing urge to leave school and find work of any kind to sustain myself. I decided, however, to hold on until I had completed my 'O' levels. It was a very difficult decision on my part to give up doing 'A' levels and forgo becoming a School Teacher. Desmond, a very good friend who was in my class at that time, continued to do his 'A' levels eventually going for Teacher Training at Hillside Teacher Training College and ending up as a Teacher in Canada.

At the end of 1965, I quit school after I wrote my "O" levels. I left school with little hope of securing a good job because Ian Smith, and his racist Cabinet had just declared independence to consolidate his minority white rule. With the country's isolation from the world looming following the imposition of mandatory sanctions on Rhodesia by Britain job opportunities for Coloureds and Blacks were very limited. Even apprenticeships were difficult to come by.

In January 1966 I started to look for a job. The Mine that my father worked for would not consider me because I was Coloured. Their response to my query was that I was "over qualified". Presumably what they meant was that I was not white enough to be employed as a Technician and not black enough to be taken on as a Labourer.

One Wednesday evening I decided to go to Salisbury by train and arrived there Thursday morning. I did not know anyone in Harare at that time and did not have any money to book into a hotel; so, I remained at Salisbury Railway Station until the businesses had opened for the day. At about 8 o'clock I went to the Employment exchange in St Barbara House in Stanley Avenue. Not long after registering I was given a referral card to go and see a Mr. Stephens at Colcom Foods in Coventry Road, a meat establishment specializing in the sale of Pork products.

On arrival at Colcom I found a few other candidates waiting to be interviewed; one of whom was a friend of mine from Embakwe. His name was Walter. We were called, one at a time, to Mr Stephens's office.

When it was my turn, I was escorted to the office and politely asked to sit on a chair opposite Mr. Stephens. After exchanging the usual pleasantries, he asked me the following question, "If you sell a dozen packets of pork sausages at three shillings and eleven and a half pence (3s 11½d), what will be the total cost of the sausages?" I replied, without any hesitation, stated that the total cost would amount to two pounds seven shillings and sixpence (£2 7s 6d). Mr Stephens was very impressed by my quick response. At the end of the interview he asked me to call him that afternoon at 2 o'clock. At precisely 2 o'clock I called him and he told me to come and start work on Monday.

After the interview I walked back to the railway station as I did not have any place to go to. I did not know anybody in Salisbury. At the station I engaged in a conversation with the Railway Porters. One of the porters happened to be a brother of Jasper, a friend of mine from Embakwe. His name was Herbert. Once he became aware of my predicament he invited me to spend a night at his house in Ardbennie.

Next morning, which was a Friday, I left Herbert's home after breakfast intending to explore the Coloured Suburb of Arcadia. That afternoon, whilst passing Morgan High School, I notice that there was a group of Coloureds who belonged to a local football team, who were practicing in the grounds of the school; so I joined in to play football. I knew some of the boys in the group from Embakwe. After practice, a friend of mine, by the name of Andrew, asked me where I was living, I told him that I had nowhere to live; so he invited me to go with him to his parent's home in Highfield, an African suburb.

The next morning, which was now a Saturday, I decided to explore the Coloured suburb of Ardbennie where I bumped into Ronnie, a cousin of Yousef, my sister Ava's husband. He, too, invited me to stay with him whilst looking for my own place to live. I stayed with Ronnie for two days. The next day, Monday, Ronnie introduced me to his landlord, who happened to have a vacant property on the same premises as those occupied by Ronnie and his family, alongside Waterfalls Avenue.

The landlord's name was Mr Gulab, an Indian man. He agreed to lease the one-bedroom flat to me. He, however, wanted me to pay a month's rent in advance. However, Ronnie guaranteed payment; so, Mr Gulab allowed me to move in without payment of the deposit. The flat consisted of just the room with no kitchen or dining room. I lived in the flat for about three months. When Monday came I went to start work at Colcom, as a Dispatch Clerk, in the knowledge that I now had a place to live.

A school friend and class mate, by the name of John, who had also come in search of work in Salisbury, came and lived with me at my invitation. John was also able to find a job as a Soils Laboratory Assistant (or Mud Doctor as it was then nicknamed) in the Ministry of Roads and Road Traffic. After about a month and a half John left to live elsewhere where he had secured accommodation sharing a three-bedroom flat with other mates from Embakwe.

Whilst living at my flat I bumped into my aunt Winnie, a Ndebele woman married to a Coloured man of Chinese descent. Their house was not far from where I was living at the time. I had known Winnie whilst I was at koSingoma. She was related to me by marriage. Her younger sister had married my uncle Kesari. She offered me a room in her house for board and lodge and I accepted. I lived with her and her family until august 1966 when I received a mandatory call-up to undertake National Service at Llewellyn Barracks, about

6 miles from Bulawayo. Although we treated as second class citizens, Coloureds were conscripted to undergo compulsory military training in order to support the whites in their war against the guerrillas who were engaged in the black man's war of liberation.

In April 1966 I got a job with the Ministry of Roads and Road Traffic as Laboratory Assistant. My friend, John was already working there and had put in a good word for me; so, I got the job without any difficulty. The job involved testing various soils for their elasticity and concrete for strength, etc. for civil engineering purposes.

CHAPTER 11

The Rise of African Nationalism and the Bush War

BY THE 1950s, the black people of Southern Rhodesia were increasingly showing signs of being dissatisfied with the abusive treatment they were receiving from the white minority government. The Native Reserve Lands were overstocked and in deteriorating condition. To halt the increase in soil erosion, the government introduced the Land Husbandry Act of 1951. The bill was a total failure. It never took into contemplation the ecological diversity of the land it reallocated. The government could have rectified the problems with the Land Husbandry Act to better suit the population, but it was in the best interest of the settler population to keep the people in the reserves poor so as to maintain the unequal wealth distribution the setters so enjoyed. There was heavy opposition by both rural farmers and urban workers.

The government introduced strict apartheid in urban areas and segregated the black and white populations in hospitals, hotels and schools. It even prevented Africans from drinking alcoholic beverages. A previous piece of legislation titled The Land Apportionment Act of 1930 implemented rigid policy as regards domestic travel within the country. Blacks were required to present papers when travelling between areas. The Land Tenure Act of the same year gave better areas to white settlers and relocated Africans to poor and unproductive land; a case in point being the removal of the *Bokodo* settlement to *Jotsholo*, pushing families out of their homes.

In spite of being in the minority, white settlers were allotted 49,100,000 acres (199,000 km²), while the black majority received disproportionally small

21.1 acres (8.5 ha). In addition, blacks were relocated to areas with poor quality soils, endemic malaria, and tsetse fly infestations.

Because trade unions had limited power due to heavy government restrictions, in the cities workers had little or no control over conditions of their employment.

By 1950 the settler regime had established only twelve public schools for Black children. This was despite the fact that there was a growing educated elite of wealthy Africans developing in the cities.

The first fully fledged Black Nationalist organization to emerge in the country was the Southern Rhodesia African National Congress (SRNC) which was formed as a political party and was led by Joshua Nkomo. It was committed to the promotion of the welfare of Africans and was active from 1957 to 1959.

The SRNC established itself as a non-violent reform group acting on a platform of universal suffrage. Its aims were to end discrimination, increase the standard of living for Africans and expand the education for Africans. It took on a multi-ethnic executive membership from across the country. This made for a unified national organization, and included white members such as Guy Clutton-Brock, an anti-apartheid agriculturalist.

In 1958 Garfield Todd became an ally of the SRNC and met with them regularly. He attempted to introduce reforms to "advance gradually the rights of the 7,000,000 blacks without upsetting the rule of the 250,000 Whites." During his administration the minimum wage for Blacks was raised, restaurants and similar establishments were given the option of being multiracial and restrictions on alcohol consumption were relaxed. Todd pushed through a reform, in the summer of 1957, which would increase the number of voting Africans from 2% to 6%, much to the alarm of his party.

When Todd returned to South Rhodesia in 1958 after a one-month holiday in South Africa he discovered his cabinet had resigned in protest of his liberal policies. Only 14 of the 24 legislators in his party supported his remaining in office. Todd refused to resign. However, on 8 February, he was voted out at a United Federal Party congress and replaced by Edgar Whitehead.

On 29 February 1959 several organisations were banned by the Whitehead administration's declaration of the state of emergency and the introduction of the Unlawful Organizations Act. The legislation allowed Government seizure of property. The administration defended the bill by claiming that the SRANC had incited violence, defied government and "undermined [the] prestige of Native Commissioners and the loyalty of African Police" said a security intelligence report. 1,610 Africans were prosecuted and 1,002 were convicted under this law between 1960 and 1965.

Another piece of legislation, called The Preventative Detention Act, allowed the government to detain several hundred members of the SRANC without trial. Some members were detained for four years in shockingly insulting conditions, while white member Clutton-Brock was released in under a month. At that time Nkomo, who was attending a conference in Cairo on his way to London, was not detained. He remained in London organizing or on speaking tours to rally support until his return home on 1 October 1960.

The Whitehead administration introduced yet another piece of legislation, The Native Affairs Amendment Act, which went even further to prevent nationalist activities by banning meetings of 15 or more natives that would "undermine the authority" of the government. This prevented rural organizing, severely limited freedom of speech, and marked the end of nonviolent resistance in Southern Rhodesia. Whitehead, to appease the black elite, conceded a few liberal reforms to benefit wealthy, educated, urban Africans.

The ANC (or SRANC) was banned early in 1959. It was replaced by the National Democratic Party (NDP). Nkomo had gone to England to escape imprisonment. When he returned in 1960 he was proclaimed leader of the party. In 1961 the NDP was also banned. He then founded the Zimbabwe African People's Union (ZAPU) and became its president. He was held in detention from 1964 until 1974 by the minority government of Rhodesia and after his release he travelled extensively in Africa and Europe to promote ZAPU's goal of black majority rule in Rhodesia.

The Zimbabwe African National Union (ZANU) was formed on 8 August 1963 as a splinter group from ZAPU largely on ethnic grounds. Ndabaningi Sithole, Henry Hamadziripi, Mukudzei Midzi, Herbert Chitepo, Edgar Tekere and Leopold Takawira decided to split from ZAPU at the house of Enos Nkala in Highfield, Salisbury, and now Harare. Robert Mugabe was not present at this meeting. The founders were ostensibly, dissatisfied with the militant tactics of Nkomo. The truth, however, was that this group wanted to distant itself from the leadership of Joshua Nkomo, who was a *Ndebele*. Both organisations were, however banned in that same year and its leaders detained at *Gonkudzingwa*.

In July 1964 both organisations re-emerged with armed wings. Zimbabwe African People's Union's armed wing was called Zimbabwe People's Revolutionary Army (ZIPRA) and Zimbabwe African National Union's armed wing was called Zimbabwe African National Liberation Army (ZANLA). This was the beginning of the Second Chimurenga (aka the "Zimbabwe War of Liberation" or "the Rhodesian Bush War". Both these groups sourced their weaponry and training from communist nations such as the Soviet Union and China. They used guerrilla tactics and traditional warfare.

Meanwhile the white minority regime was continuing with its quest to gain independence from Britain. The Rhodesian government, under its new leader Ian Smith, was indignant when, amid decolonization and Harold Macmillan's "Winds of Change", less developed African colonies to the north, such as Northern Rhodesia, without comparable experience of self-rule quickly advanced to independence in the early 1960s while Rhodesia was refused sovereignty under the newly ascendant principle of "no independence before majority rule" ('NIBMAR').

Because of four decades of self-government most whites in Rhodesia felt that they were due independence. They felt that the British Government was betraying them by withholding independence. Between 1964 and 1965 a stalemate developed between the British and Rhodesian prime ministers Harold Wilson and Ian Smith. The British government insisted that the terms of independence had to be acceptable "to the people of the country as a whole". Ian Smith contended that this was met while Wilson and the Black Nationalist leaders in Rhodesia insisted it was not.

Late in October 1965 Harold Wilson proposed that the UK might safeguard future black representation in the Rhodesian parliament by withdrawing some of the colonial government's devolved powers. He then presented terms for an investigatory Royal Commission; these the Rhodesians found unacceptable. Subsequently Ian Smith and his Cabinet declared independence. Sir Humphreys Gibbs' immediate response was that this act was treasonous. He formally dismissed Smith and his government but they ignored him and, instead, appointed Clifford Du Pont as the "Officer Administering the Government" to take his place. This meant that Rhodesia had effectively cut its ties with the British government and was no longer a member of the Commonwealth.

No country recognized Rhodesia's Unilateral Declaration of Independence (UDI). The Rhodesian High Court deemed the post- UDI government legal and de jure in 1968.

Soon after the unilateral declaration of independence the United Nations applied sanctions against Rhodesia until 1979. As an economic tool intended to effect political change, sanctions had relatively limited success.

Initially, the Smith administration professed continued loyalty to Queen Elizabeth ll. However, in 1970 it abandoned its position when it declared itself a republic in an unsuccessful attempt to win foreign recognition.

The Rhodesian bush war, a guerrilla conflict between Rhodesia government and the two rival revolutionary armies, ZIPRA and ZANLA, began in earnest about two years later. In the beginning the attacks were rather sporadic and limited in scope and consequence. The war intensified in the years 1978 and 1979.

After several attempts to end the war Ian Smith agreed to an Internal Settlement with non-militant nationalists in 1978, which included Abel Muzorewa, the president of the United African National Council and Ndabaningi Sithole, the President of ZANU (Ndonga). For agreeing to participate in the transitional four-man executive, Sithole was ousted by Robert Gabriel Mugabe as leader of the Zimbabwe National Union (ZANU) which was renamed ZANU-PF. In terms of this agreement the country was reconstituted as Zimbabwe Rhodesia under black rule in June 1979. The new arrangement was rejected by the guerrillas and the International community. Zimbabwe Rhodesia revoked its UDI as a result of the continuation of the bush war and the pressure applied as part of the Lancaster House Agreement in December 1979.

Zimbabwe Rhodesia, which was an unrecognized state born out of the internal settlement existed from 1 June 1979 to 12 December 1979. Following a brief period of direct rule under the leadership of Lord Soames, the country was granted internationally recognized independence under the name "Zimbabwe" in April 1980. Mugabe became Prime Minister of the newly liberated nation.

CHAPTER 12

National Service

I RECEIVED MY CALL up papers for the 84th Intake. I left Harare with a friend of mine by the name of George. We boarded the train at 9:00 Pm in Salisbury and arrived at Llewellyn Barracks next morning. We were met by Sgt. Budd and Lance Corporal Kelly. We were made to line up and were addressed by Colour Sgt. Howell and then commanded to jump into the waiting trucks on the double.

This was the beginning of our nine months' continuous military training. We were the 84th intake conscripted to undertake nine months of military training. This was during the UDI when the country was under sanctions from Britain. The war of liberation was not yet in full swing but there were intermittent reports of skirmishes which were referred to by the Smith regime as "terrorist" incidents.

I was not at all enthusiastic about being a soldier and, least of all, fighting on the side of the white imperialist regime. At the same time, I did not cherish the idea of fighting on the other side. Blacks, in general, did not care about us Coloureds, I felt. I was here because I really did not have a choice in the matter. Refusing to comply with my call up papers would have meant losing my job with the prospect of facing possible imprisonment or both.

We had been informed that we would be joining the army's Supply and Transport Services unit (STS). Our training was to be for the duration of eight weeks after which we would be incorporated into the 11Supply and Transport Platoon (11ST Platoon) whose main function was to supply the other army units with food, building materials, equipment and any other supplies required by soldiers in the frontline. Our primary function was to drive trucks from the main centres to deliver provisions to front line bases in places like Binga, Mt. Darwin, Kariba, etc. In addition, we would be called upon to guard various installations mainly in rural places whilst the combat units, such as the Rhodesia Light Infantry (RLI) and other units, would engage the guerrillas or "terrorists" as they were then called. In short, our main role was to drive what we called RL trucks.

On arrival at the barracks we were issued with our uniforms and shown which barrack rooms we were to occupy. We were also issued with bedding and mess equipment. We were informed about drill times, meal times, guard duties and inspections, etc. We also had to endure bullying by those who came before us who were now regarded as our seniors.

Training under Sgt. Budd, our platoon Corporal, and Colour Sgt. Howell, our platoon Sergeant, was very rigorous. We spent many hours both on the parade ground, the assault course, rifle range and on route marches. Everything we did was on the march or on the run. We were soon able to distinguish between an officer and a non-commissioned officer as failure to do so would render us liable to a charge which would, invariably, result in one having to pay a fine which would be deducted from one's pay. We were required to salute when coming across an officer. It didn't matter how many times you came across the same officer; you were still expected to salute. We were able to distinguish an officer from other ranks by a pip or pips worn on the shoulder.

If you came across a non-commissioned officer, you were expected to brace yourself and greet. A non-commissioned officer was any soldier from the level of Lance corporal to a sergeant major or Warrant Officer wearing rank stripes on the shoulder or a crown on the wrist.
As a soldier you had no choice but to tolerate the use of foul language on you. It did not matter how cooperative you behaved the platoon leaders would always use foul language on you.

On the first day at Llewellyn Barracks we were kept busy polishing the barrack room floors and windows, polishing and shining our boots, and ironing our drill khakis. The following day we were smartly dressed waiting for inspection. After this we were marched to the parade grounds to begin our drill training which would last some weeks.

Our nine-month military training was divided into phases; drill, map reading, fitness and weapon training after which we were separated to specialize in one of the following disciplines: truck driving, Signals, Medics,

Mechanics and Trackers. I was assigned to join the Medical Corps and the Tracking Unit.

As a Medic I was trained in all aspects of dealing with trauma and required to pass the Medical Assistant III (MA3) course. I also undertook a Tracking Proficiency test.

Sgt. Budd and CSgt. Howell were our drill instructors and had an amazing sense of humour. In our squad we had one recruit by the name of Private West. Pte. West could not stand up upright. His posture was such that when marching he would appear to be stooping or leaning forward. Colour Sgt Howell observed Pte. West march for some time and repeatedly asked him to walk upright. Suddenly he brought our squad to a halt, walked over to the hanger, came out whistling softly and brandishing a broom, walked towards where Pte. West was standing, thrust the top end of the broom into his shirt at the back and right down into the rear of his pants in an effort to straighten his posture to 90 degrees. He then resumed marching the squad. The whole incident was so amusing that we started to laugh uncontrollably unable to continue marching through laughter. Needless to say, we were all put under a charge.

For our fitness training we were made to endure arduous runs covering 26 miles, or more sometimes, carrying heavy back-packs. We were also required to undertake assault courses on a regular basis.

Our weapons training involved learning how to strip, clean, re- assemble and use FN FAL, FN MAG, G3, SLR and SMG 9mm machine gun. We also practiced throwing grenades. This, again, was a rigorous test of skill involving pitting our individual abilities against each other at the rifle range. Emphasis of our training was always focused on safety. Although I had not held a gun before I turned out to be one of the top marksmen in my group.

As new recruits we were subjected to all manner of bullying by our seniors. Bullying tactics ranged from being subjected to washing socks, washing trays or mess tins after meals, polishing boots, making beds and running errands for our seniors.

I remember one individual in particular who made my life a living hell. His name was Eliab. He was tall and well-built having spent a great deal of time, spanning a few months long before our call up, in detention or DB, for unspecified offences. Everybody feared him. He had targeted me from the first day that I had set foot in the camp.

Not a day would pass without him getting me to carry out his chores such as washing his socks, polishing his boots and washing his food tray after meals. No matter what I did I could not avoid this man and I resigned myself to accepting his bullying for the rest of my call-up period.

Every weekend, without fail, he would come to our barrack room purely to enjoy the pleasure of harassing us and me, in particular. Every Saturday afternoon he would come to our barrack room. He would strip all his clothes, save for his underpants, sit on a chair, and get one of us to fan him using a food tray whilst he dictated letters to his girlfriends in Civvy Street. His favourite scribe or secretary was a chap by the name of Majid. In the evenings, after harassing us, he would leave our barrack room until the following Saturday.

One evening on a Sunday, I was busy polishing my boots in the barrack room. I was preparing for Monday morning's inspection. Eliab walked into the room to perform his usual bullying. Suddenly and unexpectedly he threw his heavy boot at me. The boot struck my head against a corner of my metal locker. I experienced severe pain. On reflex I jumped on to the top of my bed and swung my right hand. My fist connected him squarely on his temple. The next thing I saw was that he had fallen and was lying sprawled on the ground and unconscious.

My reaction had not been pre-meditated as I had acted on reflex. I would not have reacted this way if I had taken some time to think about the consequences for he was a very strong person and I feared him.

The Regimental Police arrived shortly at the scene and we were both taken to detention where we were to spend the night pending a charge of disturbing the peace.

When we arrived at the so called "box" we were given beds in the same room. Reality began to dawn on me. I thought to myself, "He is going to kill me, tonight!" for he was physically stronger than I was and the only reason I knocked him out was because I had taken him by surprise and punched him in the temple which is probably the weakest part of the skull. I guess he did not feel the same way about me because, to my relief and surprise, he spoke to me very nicely making suggestions on what we should say in our defence when we would both appear before Major Francis, the officer commanding, in the morning.

After this incident I was regarded a hero. From that day until I passed out of the army I was never bullied. Little did the other soldiers realize that my knocking out Eliab was a complete fluke. I had not intended to hit him on the temple but had intuitively lashed out. I had not intended to hit him on the temple but had intuitively lashed out. My victory over Eliab was spread far and wide and, often, I would hear people say to one another as I passed-by the Coloured suburb of Barham Green, "That's the guy who knocked out Eliab". This made me feel good and secure. Furthermore, I had been promoted to the rank of Corporal due to my Tracking and Map Reading skills.

Whilst still on my National Service I received word from my sister Ava, informing me that her marriage to Yousef had irrevocably ended. She had returned from Zambia and was now living in Shabani with her three children. She wanted some money so that she could take her children to Salisbury and find work. I sent her £40.00 and she took the train and found work in Salisbury.

After completing my National Service, I returned to Harare to resume my employment with the Ministry of Roads and Road Traffic. I was pleasantly surprised to discover that, during the whole period of my National Service, my salary had been paid into my bank account. I now had a reasonable bank balance to get on with my life. As I didn't have any form of transport, I decided to buy myself a little Motor Cycle, a Yamaha 100 cc which I used to visit my father in Shabani, now and again, to find out how he was getting on.

In December of that year I received word from Shabani that my step mother had again given birth to a second baby girl. I was not at all enthusiastic about this birth as I felt that my father was too old to be having children. "Who is going to look after those children when he dies", I thought, "This will become a burden to me". Nevertheless, there was nothing I could do about it. My father was obsessed about having another son. I knew that he would continue to have children until he had a boy.

My father remained in Shabani until his retirement in late 1967. As he did not have anywhere to retire to, Ava and I made arrangement for him to come to Harare where we arranged accommodation for him and his family in the Coloured suburb of Ardbennie. We also arranged for him to receive a government pension. For his services at Shabanie Mine he was given an Omega watch after completing 25 years of service. Whilst living in Ardbennie, my father had two more children. The girl was born February 1970 and the boy was born December 1973. My father was widowed when Emma, died in 1975.

After completion of the National Service we were inducted into the Territorial Army. We were subjected to periodic call ups lasting six weeks at a time. As ours was a transport unit our role involved carrying infantry troops to strategic areas of the conflict as well as transporting supplies such as building material, rations, water, ammunition, etc. In my case, however, I would be assigned or seconded to an infantry unit such as the Rhodesia Light Infantry for the duration of my call up and employed as a Tracker. Sometimes I would take the roll of medic if assigned to a unit where there was no medic.

CHAPTER 13

My Employment and Marriage

ON MY RETURN from the army I shared a two bedroomed flat with Andrew a friend from my school days. Our flat was at Gorlon House in Stanley Avenue. Andrew was popular and had many girl friends who would visit our flat over weekends and public holidays and, as a result, there was never a dull moment.

I used to park my motorcycle in a park space under the building next to a fellow tenant by the name of Peter. Sometimes I would bump into Peter and his wife as they left for work in the morning. Peter and his wife would sometimes give a lift to a nice-looking girl. I did not know this girl but whenever our eyes met I could feel the mutual attraction. I made no attempt to make her acquaintance because, by nature, I am an introvert.

I became somewhat disillusioned with having a motorcycle as my main mode of transportation. I did not particularly enjoy getting wet during the rainy season; so, I decided to invest in an old Morris Minor sedan. It was a non-runner and needed fixing. I did not know how to fix cars and I didn't have the money to hire a mechanic. I had a very good friend, by the name of Kamal, to help me fix the car and all I had to do was buy spare parts.

My sister, Ava and her family lived at Bamawa House in Rotten Row about half a kilometre away. At Bamawa House there was a yard where we could park the car and repair it. My friend Kamal and I were busy fixing the car when the same girl, whom I had seen on several previous occasions, waiting for a lift at Gorlon House, passed us on her way to her flat from work. Like my sister she also had a flat at Bamawa House. The next day she passed by again but this time I plucked up courage, approached her, introduced myself and asked her if she would come with me to the cinema to watch a movie, titled the *"Odd Couple"*, starring Jack Lemon and Walter Matthau. The following week I asked her, once again, to go out with me to watch another movie entitled "To Sir with Love" starring Sydney Poitier. That was the beginning of our romance and courtship that ended in us moving in to live together.

During our courtship I discovered that Veronica and I had a lot in common. Veronica comes from a large family – 3 brothers, 4 half- brothers, 1 sister, 3 half- sisters and two step-sisters. She was born at *eNkankezi*, not far from where my father had set up his home when he married my mother. Her mother was a *Ndebele* from the *Venda* tribe and her father was Coloured like my father. Our paternal grandfathers were pioneers who had fought in the *Matabele Rebellion*. We were both fluent in the *Ndebele* and *Shona* languages.

In addition, I found Veronica to be a caring, loving and a selfless person. At that time my father was living in Ardbennie with his young family surviving on a paltry pension. She would often remind me of my obligation to assist in order to alleviate their suffering. I would often complain that my father had himself to blame for his suffering as he should not be still fathering children at his age. She would ask me to be tolerant and continue to assist whenever I could.

When I moved in to live with Veronica I was just twenty years old and she was twenty-one. On 24 March 1973 we married in a private ceremony attended by a very few close friends.

The flat that we rented became small and, after the birth of our first child in February 1970, we moved to a Coloured suburb of Sunningdale. It is while we were living in Sunningdale that our twin girls were born in August 1973. Sharon, one of the twins, died in November 1974 from a measles complication.

When Sharon died we were distraught. I can still recall Veronica holding a prayer vigil at Sharon's hospital bedside as the child was struggling to breath for two days. She could neither eat nor drink and her condition steadily deteriorated until she died. I could neither eat nor drink nor sleep for many days. I just couldn't come to terms with what had just happened – what terrible grief. Up to now I can still picture in my mind her pretty little smiling face and her beautiful eyes.

At that time, we could only find accommodation in designated Coloured areas such as Arcadia, Sunningdale and Ardbennie in Salisbury (later Harare) and Barham Green, Trenance and Rangemore in Bulawayo. You could not choose to live in such suburbs as Greendale as these were specifically set aside as white residential areas. There were, also, high density areas such as Highfield in Salisbury (Harare) and Mpopoma in Bulawayo. Coloureds could neither rent nor buy in the black or white areas.

In 1975, whilst living in Sunningdale, we were able to buy a piece of land and build a house in the new suburb of St Martins. It was a three- bedroomed house to which we added another bedroom to accommodate our growing family.

I worked as a Soils Laboratory Assistant for some months and later transferred to the Ministry of Roads Training Centre were I was employed as an Administrative Cadet. I remained in this position until 1 July 1967 when I took a lateral transfer to the Ministry of Roads and Road Traffic's Head Office which was situated in Coghlan House, 4th Street, Salisbury.

It was when we were still living in our new house in the suburb of St. Martins that Genevieve was born in December 1977. By this time Veronica was experiencing some health challenges. It was time to stop having any more children.

My desire at this point in my life was to pursue a career in the Civil Service. I had been made to understand that, theoretically, one could advance within the Civil Service up to the grade of Secretary and become a head of a government department or ministry. To achieve this one had to pass the Public Services Diploma in Public Administration. This diploma was split into three modules – Preliminary Diploma, Intermediate Diploma and Final Diploma.

After successfully completing the Preliminary Diploma you became eligible for advancement to the grade of Administrative Assistant. I completed the Preliminary Diploma in Public Administration in May 1970 and was promoted to the grade of Administrative Assistant. I was employed in the Personnel Department responsible for staff recruitment, staff terminations, conditions of service, etc. This involved liaising with various departmental heads with regards to staff interviews, staff selection, staff development and appointments, etc.

In about May 1973 I completed the Intermediate Diploma in Public Administration. Completion of the Intermediate Diploma entitled me to be considered for the position of Administrative Officer. After an interview with the Public Services Commission I was given the promotion within my current ministry i.e. the Ministry of Roads and Road Traffic. I was employed in the legal aspects of administration specializing in the declaration of roads and road closures focusing on the aspects of compensation.

Although I had passed the diploma in May 1973, I was only promoted to my new position in July 1975. I was superseded several times as preference was always given to white candidates because of racialism within the Rhodesia Public Service.

Completion of the Final Diploma would result in one becoming eligible for appointment to the post of Senior Administrative Officer. Progression beyond this grade was solely depended upon availability of senior positions in the civil service.

It must be noted here that passing the Public Services Diploma did not constitute a rapid advancement if you were non-white or Coloured. I was superseded by whites, on several occasions, despite having been given excellent performance reports by my immediate supervisors.

In May 1976 I completed my Diploma in Public Services Administration gained promotion to the grade of Senior Administrative Officer within the Ministry of Roads and Road Traffic the same year.

My prospects for promotion improved dramatically from 1976 when the guerrilla war began to escalate and intensify and the whites were leaving Rhodesia in droves to settle overseas and South Africa. It was during this period of uncertainty that I started to feel that I needed to obtain a degree in accountancy and administration and I enrolled with the Rapid Results College and Salisbury Polytechnic and registered to study for the Institute of Chartered Secretaries and Administrators. I studied at night whilst working during the day and this qualified me to later start my own accounting and secretarial business.

A major portion of my career was spent working for the Ministry of Roads and Road Traffic during which period I gained extensive experience in personnel, accounting and legal fields. I transferred to the Ministry of Defence in 1977 where I dealt extensively with compensation claims relating to the servicemen killed or wounded on active service, accommodation and the drafting of Executive Orders, Minutes, etc. which would be checked by the Government Law Officers and signed by the President.

During my employment in the Ministry of Roads and Road Traffic, for the most part, my white colleagues made me feel comfortable to the extent that, at times I forgot that I was a Coloured surrounded by a "sea" of White colleagues. However, there were times that I would be jolted into reality by insensitive comments.

One day a very senior colleague with whom I used to travel to the various urban centres on business and sharing motel rooms passed a remark in an open-plan office, when speaking about a Coloured Registry Clerk who was frequently late at work, to the effect that Coloured People were unreliable. On realizing that I was present in the room, he tried to placate me by saying that his statement did not include me as I was different. This was a typical example of racism endured by non-whites during the final days of white rule.

Zimbabwe's Independence was hailed with euphoria by the African population. There was a great deal of expectation gripping the nation. Many believed that it would usher in untold prosperity and freedom from oppression.

The white population, on the other hand, viewed Independence, as an end to their privileged life. There was a surge in emigration to such countries as the UK, Australia and South Africa. From a peak population of 250,000, the population had dwindled to less than 200,000 by the middle of 1975. At one time before Independence, there were more white people that you would find in First Street than Black people. In the civil service, which was staffed mainly by the whites, there was a steady stream of them leaving their jobs.

It was a time of uncertainty for me and my family and other Coloureds employed in the Civil Service. For the previous six months leading to independence rumours had been circulating that, as one of the new government's priorities, it would introduce legislation directing that all vacant posts be filled by Indigenous Africans. This meant that, in my case, any position above my current grade of Senior Administrative Officer would have to be filled by an African. This resulted in my later leaving the Civil Service after some 15 years of service, to seek employment opportunities elsewhere.

In April 1980 I was nominated to be part of the Independence Celebrations Committee. I and a few other members, all of them white, were tasked with organizing the Banquet at the Meikles Hotel. The Banquet was attended by Prince Charles, as the guest of honour and representative of the

Queen, Lord Soames, as the Interim Governor of Rhodesia, and all heads of commonwealth governments and other dignitaries.

Our primary task was to arrange the seating of all the delegates in accordance with protocol. As each dignitary arrived we would greet them and escort them to their seats. We had arranged the seating in such a manner as to ensure that the heads of state, whose countries did not have good relations, were not seated next to each other. For example, we made certain that the leader of the Palestinian Liberation Organization (PLO), Yasser Arafat, was not seated next to the Israeli Prime Minister, Menachem Begin.

Other members of the Independence Celebrations Committee were assigned to organize seating for dignitaries and invited guests at Rufaro Stadium. Attendance or admission to Rufaro Stadium, which was strictly controlled, was by invitation only. This decision had been taken because the country did not have a large enough stadium to accommodate all the people who wished to attend.

In order to enable the general public to witness the event as it was taking place, it was broadcast live on television and radio. Friday April 18 and Saturday April 19 were declared public holidays so that everyone could take part in the celebrations.

Prince Charles, heir to the British throne, presided over the independence ceremony which marked the ending of 90 years of white domination and 15 years of illegal independence. The celebrations began at midnight with the lowering of the Union Jack for the last time and the raising of the new five-coloured Zimbabwe flag.

In the speech that he wrote the prime minister, Robert Mugabe, said "If yesterday I fought you as an enemy, today you have become a friend and ally with the same national interest, loyalty, rights and duties as myself. If yesterday you hated me, today you cannot avoid the love that binds you to me to you."

In a speech echoing Mugabe's theme of reconciliation Prince Charles drew cheers from the crowd when he used a Shona word for independence. Lord Carrington, the British Foreign Secretary, read a message from Prime Minister Margaret Thatcher in which she pledged close cooperation in helping the development and reconstruction of the country

Among the VIPs to witness the ceremony were the Indian Prime Minister Indira Ghandi, Pakistani President Mohammed Zia ulHaq, Australian Prime Minister Malcolm Fraser, to name just a few. Several African presidents and the United Nations Secretary General Kurt Waldheim also attended.

Joshua Nkomo, a guerrilla leader and Mugabe's main rival, was emotional with what appeared to be tears in his eyes as the new flag went up. Absent from the ceremony was former Prime Minister Ian Smith. He was on a lecture tour of South Africa.

For the African continent and its people, Zimbabwe's independence represented a high-water mark in its effort to achieve majority rule. The main problem for the new leadership was to bind emotional wounds of a war that had killed at least 50,000 people and rebuild the country where hundreds of schools, clinics and hospitals were destroyed and more than a million people had been left homeless.

Since his election Mugabe had downplayed his Marxist leanings whilst seeking to build bridges to the west. He noted that the country's greatest need was for outside assistance and stated, "We have certainly won the goodwill of many countries and can confidently expect to benefit from the economic and technical aid they are able and willing to provide for us."

While assuring the population of 200,000 whites that there would be no retaliation for past injustices inflicted upon his people, he said his government was determined to bring about "meaningful change to the lives of the majority of the people." He, however, cautioned the blacks not to expect immediate change.

After the formal ceremony had ended, the late Jamaican superstar, Bob Nester Marley graced the occasion, churning out songs from his "Survival" album. During the show, which lasted 30 minutes, he sang: "War", "No more Trouble", "Chant Down Babylon", "Blackman Redemption", "Get Up. Stand Up (for your rights)", and of course, "Zimbabwe" and the whole nation went ecstatic.

The following day all the heads of state and Government and all of us, members of the Independence Celebrations Committee, were invited to state house. On the grounds of State House, we mingled with the entire group of invited guests. I particularly remember chatting with Andrew Young, who was at that time, United States Ambassador to the United Nations, and Ghanaian

President, Flight Lieutenant Jerry Rawlings.

Soon after Independence I was introduced to Rex Nhongo (a.k.a. Solomon Mujuru). He had come to see me at my office at Milton Buildings. He wanted me to organize accommodation for some of the ZANLA personnel. Allocating accommodation for army personnel was part of my responsibilities. From then on whenever he wanted accommodation for his cadres he would send someone to come and see me. Despite our introduction, whenever he sent someone, he would tell them to come and ask for, "*Mukomana mutsuku*" which means in Shona 'a light skinned young man'. Never at any time did he address me by my proper name and this annoyed me greatly.

In October 1980 Rex Nhongo came by my office so I could accompany him to Harare Airport as a representative of the Ministry of Defence. We were going to welcome a contingent of North Korean Army personnel who had arrived in Zimbabwe to oversee the establishment and training of the Fifth Brigade.

Prime Minister Robert Mugabe had signed an agreement with the North Korean President, Kim ll Sung, in October 1980. The terms of the agreement were that North Korea would train and equip a brigade for the Zimbabwe National Army (ZNA). 106 North Koreans arrived to train the new brigade in August, 1981.

Fifth Brigade members were drawn from 3,500 former troops of the Zimbabwe African National Army (ZNLA) which included two unintegrated ZANLA Battalions at *Tongogara* Assembly Point. Initially there were a few Zimbabwe People's Revolutionary Army (ZIPRA) troops but these were withdrawn before training was completed.

Little did I realize, at the time that in accompanying Rex Nhongo to welcome the North Koreans I was party to the establishment of *Gukurahundi*. This has had a profound effect upon me in that this action brought a great tribulation to the Ndebele people of Matabeleland.

The *Gukurahundi*, which means "the early rain which washes away the chaff before the spring rains" represents a sad phase in the history of Zimbabwe. Established as the Fifth Brigade and headed by Brigadier Perence Shiri, *Gukurahundi* was a series of massacres of more than 20,000 Ndebele civilians, some of whom were close relatives of mine. As time progressed I began to feel disgruntlement. I was disgruntled because there were no longer any prospects of advancement or promotion in the Civil Service unless you were a Black African. I was disgruntled because I was being drawn closer to ZANU-PF hierarchy through my work association with Nhongo. I became convinced that I was treading on dangerous ground and that it was time to move on. I decided then to find another job.

I put out my CV and the only decent job I could get was with the Agricultural Development Authority (ADA) as a Budget Controller. I was not really keen on this position because ADA was a quasi- government entity which meant it would be tainted by politics. As I really did not have any choice I took the job.

It was about at this time that I started to think very seriously of working for myself – but how? What could I successfully do on my own?

At this time ADA was still run by white people but the General Manager was Black and the Board Chairman was white.

It was not very long before the whites left and replaced by blacks. By then I had been promoted to the position of Administration Controller/ Company Secretary, a position I held until my resignation in 1988 when I went into private practice as an accountant.

Another tragic event took place in our lives. We lost Bernard, Veronica's son and my step-son, to cancer. He had been diagnosed with cancer on his right knee. He was in the prime of his life having started his career in the Zimbabwe Republican Police. He was only twenty-seven years old. When the tumor was discovered it was too late and the chemotherapy did not work. The hospital had sent him home to die. This was another very sad moment in our lives. I could see only anguish in Veronica's eyes as she faced the task of nursing her son knowing that her efforts would ultimately end in his death. At first we found it very difficult to reconcile ourselves to the fact that we were about to lose another sibling in a space of twenty years.

I tried to be very supportive to Bernard as much as I could be under the circumstances. I read to him messages of hope from the Bible and prayed for him and with him, for my wife and the other siblings. We had Counsellors from Island Hospice come by the house to show us how to administer morphine and how to make him as comfortable as possible. We also had support from our local Seventh-Day Adventist Church. They would visit and take time praying for Bernard and singing hymns. Sadly, Bernard died at home on 3 January 1993.

Sometime in the early 1990s when looking at Veronica I was perturbed to notice that her eyes were somewhat bulging and appearing open in a wide-eyed stare. She no longer looked like the same person that I had married. Her look reminded me of a woman, with whom we attended church, who had been diagnosed with hyperthyroidism. I did not give the matter much thought but, at the back of my mind I suspected that Veronica may be suffering from hyperthyroidism.

For the next ten years Veronica faced a succession of health challenges. She had a series of surgical interventions, including a twisted bowel (twice), gall stones, appendicitis (which had relocated from its normal positioning) and kidney stones. I had been told and had read somewhere that thyroid malfunctions can cause damage to the various systems and organs of the body, including the cardiovascular system. Before each operation I had suggested to the physicians that the causes leading to the operation may have been the thyroid malfunction but my suggestions were either rejected or ignored.

Veronica was in constant pain. She suffered severe pain on her shoulders, neck and spinal cord. The disease seemed to come up at night as soon as the sun went down and would ease in the morning when the sun came up. Doctor Forbes thought that she was suffering from fibromyalgia and put her on steroids. This did not help at all.

Veronica's health continued to deteriorate with the passage of time. Although the doctors could not pin point the source of her illness it was clear that she was suffering from an unspecified autoimmune disease.

In 1997 we had a visit from our friends, Gilbert and Glynnis, who had, two years before, migrated to New Zealand. They were both RNs. After taking one look at Veronica, Glynnis suggested that she might be suffering from a thyroid disorder.

At our next doctor's visit I, again, suggested to the doctor that Veronica may be suffering from a thyroid disorder. This time he did not rebuff me but, arranged for her to have a blood test. I asked him why, unlike on a previous occasion, he had accepted my suggestion? He replied saying that, because he had not known her for long, he could not tell from looking at her eyes, that her eyes were bulging. The test confirmed that she was suffering from hyperthyroidism. She was put on an antithyroid drug therapy treatment. She began to suffer from side effects resulting in abnormal hair loss, insomnia or sleeplessness, muscle and joint aches.

Because of the deteriorating economic situation in the country we decided to go and work in the UK. My accounting business was no longer doing well because of the white farm invasions that were affecting many of my clients. On the other hand, black entrepreneurs, who were now beginning to dominate the small businesses, were keen to introduce creative accounting; the concept of which was the exploitation of loopholes in financial regulations in order to gain advantage or present figures in a misleadingly favourable light.

Our plan was to work in the UK so we could pay-off our daughter's college fees. She was at Oakwood University in Huntsville, Alabama. She was mid-way through her Bio-Chemistry degree course. Failure to pay the fees would have meant her returning to Zimbabwe without completing her degree.

Although she was very sickly by now Veronica decided to come to England to help me work to raise the fees. The idea was that we would work, pay-off the debt and return to Zimbabwe within a period of two years.

I went to London in May 2000. Veronica followed in August. Her symptoms improved somewhat and she was able to work. She seemed to thrive in cold weather. She was able to continue until the end of 2010 when she retired and migrated to Australia.

In London, the Endocrinologist first thought of surgically removing Veronica's gland but later decided on radioactive iodine treatment. After the treatment her condition changed from being over active to under active. This resulted in her remaining on thyroxin indefinitely.

Veronica continues to suffer from the autoimmune syndrome. This illness erupts from time to time. In 2007 she was diagnosed with a leaky valve. This causes shortness of breath, leg swelling, fluid retention, heart fluttering or palpitations and fatigue. Here in Australia her condition is monitored on a six monthly basis.

CHAPTER 14

Ava's Marriage

WHEN AVA LEFT *koSingoma* after her quarrel with my aunt, she was enrolled and attended Jeffrey Hooper School. On arrival at this school she was placed in a class in which most of the pupils were much younger than she was. Disgruntled she left the school to seek employment, without completing her primary education. She took a job at a bakery out of town.

In 1958 Ava met and married a Coloured man by the name of Yousef. He was employed as a Grader Operator by the Roads Department. After their marriage they lived at a roads department camp which was about twenty-five miles from Beitbridge along the road to Fort Victoria (now Masvingo).

Ava's marriage to Yousef seemed to go well at the beginning. In May of 1959 Ava became pregnant with her first-born son. Yousef brought her to our home in Shabani so she could give birth at the newly built Coloured hospital. Ava had to give birth by Caesarean section which meant she had to remain in Shabani for some time.

It was agreed that I should return to the road department camp with Joseph until Ava's return with her new born baby. It was during my stay that I discovered Yousef's character and habits. His behaviour made me realise that their marriage was just a sham and would not last. Yousef loved women. He drank excessively and used drugs and he was a spendthrift.

During my short stay with him we spent lots of time at the local Venda Village partying with lots of liquor being consumed. He was a polished guitarist and was popular with the ladies. At the end of the day a woman would come home with us to spend the night and even cook breakfast for us.

This happened every weekend until Ava's return. When I returned to my father in Shabani I recounted my experience with Yousef and told him that I didn't think that Ava's marriage would last.

After the birth of Ava's first born child, Yousef's behaviour began to change remarkably. In addition to drunkenness and drug use, he became very abusive to Ava. When drunk he would pick a fight with her to get some pretext to leave the house so that he could go and be with his girlfriends.

As things got worse I would encourage Ava to leave Yousef before they could have more children. The problem was that she had no one to leave her son with and find employment. She could not leave her son with my father because he did not have a wife and I was still going to school and could not help in looking after him.

Despite the deteriorating conditions Ava clung on to her marriage hoping that Yousef's behaviour would change for the better. This was, in my opinion, a very big mistake.

Inevitably Ava fell pregnant again and again and had to leave Yousef behind on the Roads Department to go and give birth. On both occasions when he was left alone he ran out of money and sold a Sewing Machine at one time and some other household item at another time to get a drink or a "fix". He had many African friends because he ran a little side business whereby he would help them to acquire liquor from bottle stores or other liquor retail outlets at a fee. At that time non- whites were, by law, not permitted to purchase liquor without a license. Somehow Yousef had acquired a liquor licence.

Ava persevered in her marriage and stayed with her husband for as long as she could. She had a total of three children by him, two boys and a girl, all born by Caesarean section.

Whilst at Embakwe early in 1963, I received news that Yousef had left his job and moved to Kitwe in Northern Rhodesia (now Zambia). As this was still during the Federation of Rhodesia and Nyasaland Yousef had not needed a passport to go to Northern Rhodesia. By the time Ava and her children followed her husband in February 1964, the Federation had been dissolved and she had to have a passport to crossover to the new country of Zambia.

Yousef had not been expecting Ava to follow him so when she arrived she found that he was living with a Zambian woman. After some disagreement they managed to get rid of the woman and make up. Everything went back to normal until one day in late 1966, Yousef, without any warning, told his family to pack as they were now returning to Rhodesia.

When they arrived at Yousef's cousin's home in Lusaka, Yousef pretended that he was going to the Rhodesian Embassy to apply for a passport to enable him to return to Rhodesia. Yousef had entered the country before independence and had not needed a passport to travel in and out until now. Yousef did not return from the Embassy and was not heard of again. After a while Ava realised that she had been abandoned and decided to make her way to Rhodesia with her children.

She had no money for Yousef had left her with just enough money to get her to Shabani. At this time, I was undergoing National Service at Llewellyn Barracks just outside Bulawayo. Because she desperately needed money I sent her £40 by postal order. With this money she was able to go to Salisbury where she found a job at Helvey Knitwear making Sweaters and other woolen products. Fortunately for Ava our cousin Esther, Aunt Ruth's daughter, was working in Salisbury living in Ardbennie where she was able to offer Ava and her three children temporary accommodation when seeking employment.

When she settled in Salisbury she was able to support herself and her children and to send them to Moffat Primary School and, later, Morgan High School. Sometime later she received news that Yousef was seriously ill in Zambia. She and her sister-in-law went to *Solwezi* in Zambia, where he had moved, hoping that they could, perhaps, bring him back to Rhodesia. When they arrived at *Solwezi* they were told that Yousef had died the day before they had arrived. He died in 1972 at the age of 38.

Ava continued to work and to care for her children. It was a continuous struggle taking care of three growing children with very little income. Sometime in 1967 Ava met and lived with a Spaniard by the name Alejandro. He was good to her and her children. In fact, he was instrumental in helping us to relocate our father from Shabani to Salisbury. We were able to find a place for my father to rent. We also arranged for my father to receive a government funded old age pension. At the time the Rhodesian administration of Ian Smith had a scheme whereby the aged Whites and Coloureds were given a pension. Had there not been such a scheme in place it would have been very difficult for us to take care of our father and his family.

Unbeknown to Ava, Alejandro had a girlfriend. One day a woman came carrying a baby to Bamawa House where Alejandro and Ava were living, and handed the baby to Alejandro and said to him, "Take and look after your child". This incident ended the relationship and on that day Alejandro left and he has not been seen since.

Ava met Victor and married him sometime in 1975. He was an Englishman born in Ipswich, England. Early in his life he played football for Ipswich Town Football Club. He came to Rhodesia in 1972 via South Africa where he spent some time. At the time he met Ava he was a coach for Arcadia United, which was a quite popular football team at the time. Ava and Vic bought a house in Cranborne. Vic worked at Colcom until his retirement in 1990.

Her daughter always felt that her losing her father was her mother's fault.

She had a son by her first marriage. The marriage did not last and she soon had a second son from another relationship and his name was Marvin.

After Marvin was born it was discovered that he could not speak and do anything that a normal child can do. As he grew it became evident that he needed special care. Because of his disability, Marvin requires special care which only a loving, understanding and dedicated person can give. I salute my sister Ava for her patience and dedication which she has shown by caring for Marvin these past thirty years.

Not long after her marriage to Vic, Ava took three of her grandchildren, including Marvin and looked after them in Cranborne. She fostered them because she loved them very much.

In 1992 Vic decided to return to the UK, taking with him his wife and the three adopted grandchildren. This was a grand gesture which would ensure that the two boys would have a great start in life and Marvin would be taken care of. Remaining in Zimbabwe would have been a total disaster for the two boys, due to the state of the economy, as there was no opportunity for them to start a new life there. As for Marvin, Ava loved her grandson so much that she was unwilling to part with him despite the struggles associated with providing and taking care of him.

The fact that Ava has been taking care of Marvin for over thirty years testifies of her love, patience and devotion. I can think of no other person that can do such a selfless act as Ava did under such trying circumstances. I recall how she would patiently wait for Marvin to get through his rituals before using the toilet after which she would proceed to clean him up and place him in the bath tub to bathe him.

For some inexplicable reason her daughter does not seem to appreciate what her mother has been doing for her. She does not appreciate the sacrifices that Ava has been making to look after her son. Ava is getting on in age. The time is coming that she will no longer be capable of taking care of Marvin. I shudder to think of what will happen when Ava dies over in England. Who will take care of Marvin?

My hope and prayer is that she will be able to find a good care home to look after Marvin. He is such a sweet young man. My heart goes out to him.

CHAPTER 15

Territorial Service

AFTER COMPLETING NATIONAL Service, I was not called up for Territorial Army Service until November 1973. By this time, I had married and had young children. Veronica and I had just had twin girls in August of that year. The war of liberation had begun to intensify. I just did not cherish the idea of taking up arms to prop up the Smith regime. I did not wish to die for the white man's selfish cause. Besides, God had blessed me with beautiful twin girls and I was fond and loved them dearly and wanted to take care of them. I could not bear the thought of being killed in the army and leaving them without a father.

I worked on a strategy to get myself out of the army altogether. I reported for my call-up along with the other men. I dared not refuse or stay away for fear of losing my job or imprisonment or both. We arrived at Inkomo Barracks for induction which included medical check-ups, weapon and fitness training, etc. For my medical check-up, one of the requirements was for me to provide a urine sample. Alone in the bathroom I spiced the sample with a tablespoon full of sugar that I had brought with me from the mess room.

After my medical I continued to take part in training and the refresher courses. However, before we were deployed to the Zambezi Valley, I was called to the Officer Commanding's Office I was informed that I was being demobilized because I was suspected of suffering from sugar diabetes. I was elated and overjoyed so much that when I returned home I celebrated my freedom with my very close friends.

I did not receive another call-up for the next three years or so. I thought that I may have fallen off the Army's radar as I was not receiving any call-ups whilst all my friends were receiving regular call-ups. I was very confident that I would never receive a call-up as I was convinced that I had beaten the system.

I was very surprised and disappointed to receive a call-up early in 1977. I protested claiming that I had been discharged on medical grounds and that I was not fit to undertake military service. The army would not buy my story and I was ordered to undertake a medical examination after which I joined the others on call-up. There were many other call-ups that followed.

There is one call-up that remains etched in my mind. For this call-up we were deployed in the Makuti area of Mashonaland West Province. Our Platoon Sergeant Major was a chap by the name of Aziz.

Our base camp was in a Roads Department camp in the middle of a game reserve. I remember seeing three lion cubs lying on the side of the road with their mother as we passed by on the road to the camp site. Later that night we could hear the roar of lions in the distance.

I was assigned to share a room with a chap by the name of Victor. He was a very fair Coloured who could be mistaken for a white person if it were not for his features. He was very fluent in the Shona language. Victor and I became very good friends and we were sharing a room.

Victor had brought with him a pet python which he kept in our room. I felt somewhat uneasy to share a room with a python but I had no choice in the matter. I soon got used to the idea, however.

One evening a hyena strayed into our camp grounds looking for something to scavenge. It had probably come through a hole in the perimeter fence. The guards, perhaps being bored of doing nothing, started to chase the animal. Soon others joined in and, in no time at all; the camp was abuzz with noise and excitement. The hyena could not escape for it was trapped and could not find the hole in the fence where it had got in. eventually, the hyena died from exhaustion. I was very saddened by this experience.

One evening we received a message that there had been a "terrorist" attack at a nearby camp site and several soldiers had been killed and one had survived sustaining multiple injuries. As a medic, I was asked to accompany a rescue team. On arrival I administered first aid which included giving the patient a saline drip. I strapped and secured the patient ready for evacuation to Karoi Hospital.

This was also a Coloured unit guarding the installation of a borehole. While I was attending to him I discovered that the survivor could speak and understand the isiNdebele language. He, too, became aware that I could speak the language.

As we made our way to the hospital in the back of a jeep, he recounted how his unit had come under attack from ZIPRA cadres. He survived because he had hidden himself in the undergrowth. He had heard them say to one another in Ndebele, "*Ungapi? Ungapi?*" which translates to, "Where is he? Where is he?". He lay motionless in the grass, scarcely breathing until the guerillas had departed on hearing the sound of a helicopter approaching.

The ZIPRA guerillas were very known for their aggressiveness to the extent that, on receiving call-up papers, you would be overjoyed if you were being called-up to do service in the ZANLA area of the conflict but somewhat subdued if you were called-up to undergo territorial service in the ZIPRA infested area of the conflict. A white NCO drove the jeep and I accompanied him to Karoi hospital in the dead of the night. The wounded soldier spent a few days at Karoi hospital and was subsequently transferred to Andrew Fleming hospital in Harare where he recovered fully and returned to civilian life.

My next call-up was from the middle of August to the end of September 1978. I was seconded to an infantry unit as a tracker. We were operating east of Karoi when, on 3 September 1973, we received a report that an Air Rhodesia Flight 825 was shot down by "terrorists". The Aircraft that was involved was a Vickers Viscount named the "Hunyani".

The aircraft was flying the final leg of Air Rhodesia's regular scheduled service from Victoria Falls to Salisbury, via the resort town of Kariba. As soon as the aircraft had taken-off, a group of ZIPRA guerillas hit on its starboard wing with a Soviet-made Strela- 2 surface-to air infrared homing missile critically damaging the aircraft and forcing an emergency landing.

The pilot's attempted belly landing in a cotton field just west of Karoi had been foiled by a ditch, and this had caused the plane to cartwheel and break-up, killing 38 passengers and crew. On approaching the wreckage, the insurgents rounded up the survivors they could see and massacred them with automatic gunfire. 5 Passengers lived because they had left the site to look for water before the guerrillas had arrived.

The other three passengers survived by concealing themselves in the surrounding bushes.

Our platoon was mobilized and tasked to track the insurgents. As our truck was heading towards the area of the plane crash there was a sudden explosion. The truck careered across the road and through a fence resting on a large ant-hill. The truck had detonated a landmine.

There was great confusion. We worried that a fire would break out. We scrambled to get off the truck and take cover. I jumped-off, opening fire towards the bush overgrowth as I ran. I took a position behind a small ant-hill; some 50 yards from the truck. Suddenly, everything went quiet. The insurgents had left.

All of us in the truck sustained injuries - some serious and others superficial. I had the least injury – a small bald patch at the back of my head caused by shrapnel.

After this incident a fierce white Rhodesian backlash followed with many whites becoming violently resentful and suspicious of blacks in general, even though there were few black Rhodesians who supported attacks of this kind.

Yet another Air Rhodesia Viscount was brought down by ZIPRA on 12 February, 1979. In this instance it was the Air Rhodesia Flight 827, the Umniati, a scheduled flight between Kariba and Salisbury. There were 59 people killed this time with no survivors and the circumstances were similar to those of Air Flight 825 about five months earlier.

It was, I believe, these two incidents that forced the whites to capitulate and seek a settlement that led to black majority rule. After these incidents whites began to leave the country in droves. Before these incidents, at the First Street Mall you would find a lot of whites about but after these incidents their numbers began to dwindle until there were hardly any whites by the middle of 1979.

CHAPTER 16

The Extended Family

MY FATHER, BENJAMIN Holl, died in August 1980 after a short illness. He was 74 years old. He was living in the Coloured suburb of Arcadia with his four children.

The eldest had just completed school and I had found her a job with the Ministry of Roads and Road Traffic where I had been working until my lateral transfer to the Ministry of Defence. It was because of my influence and friendship with my former colleagues that she was given a job. I had hoped that by finding her a job she would be able to take care of herself as well as contribute to the upkeep of her siblings.

Nonetheless, now that my father had died I was faced with a dilemma. Who was going to take care of these children? Since independence a few months ago the welfare system that had existed all along and had been introduced by the settler regime to cater for Coloureds and Whites alone had been discontinued as it was considered not to be in the interests of all the people in the country.

For years I had been dreading this moment for I knew that there was always the possibility that my father would die before all of his young children reached adulthood. There was absolutely nothing I could have done but hope for the best outcome. Now that he had died panic set in. "What am I going to do", I thought.

There was no other family member to turn to or share this burden with. Ava was also fostering her own grandchildren. Kathleen was preoccupied with her own problems and could not be of any help. My aunts, i.e. my father's sisters were too old to be of any help; besides they were being looked after by their adult children. "Should I look around and find an orphanage to send them to?" I thought?

Whilst I was considering my options Veronica suggested that we should, perhaps, take them in to look after them ourselves. This idea did not appeal to me at all. My recent experience was that orphaned children were seldom grateful to their benefactors. I knew of a recent case that involved our friends, Johannes and Monica, who had earlier in their lives, brought home three orphaned children to their home in Ardbennie, looked after them and nurtured them until they grew up and worked for themselves. After leaving home did they, at any time, show gratitude or thank them for fostering them? No. Johannes and his wife, Monica, lamented the fact that these children did not show any gratitude or even to send Christmas cards or even to call them to ask how they were doing.

The other thoughts that crossed my mind was how my father and his three siblings suffered and lacked education because their father neglected to ensure that they were adequately provided for after he left their mother to marry the French widow. The thought that my father's children might suffer the same fate, if we did not take them in, troubled me. It was because of these troubling thoughts that I relented and eventually agreed to take them in; a decision I have regretted all my life.

I know that, as a kind and selfless person, Veronica was thinking of the fate of the children. I do not think that, at the time, she realised the immense challenges that we would be faced with.

At that time, we were living in a house that we had built in 1975 at St. Martins, a Coloured suburb of Harare. The three-bedroomed property stood on a quarter of an acre. It had an outbuilding with two rooms. It was just big enough for our family. We therefore had no other choice but to accommodate my father's children in one of the back rooms, leaving the other room for the domestic worker. This was the best arrangement we could come to under the circumstances.

It was never our intention to segregate or to discriminate against my father's children. We just did not have enough room. We did not even have the option at the time to sell and look for another house in the community. There were no bigger or suitable houses for sale in St. Martins, Ardbennie or Arcadia. There were bigger houses in the surrounding suburbs, but these were far and few in between as this was soon after independence and the white residential areas were only beginning to open their doors to non-whites due to the new political environment.

It was very difficult for Veronica and I to cope financially with the needs of the large family. These were very stressful times. Instead of buying readymade clothes Veronica had to resort to buying a sewing machine to make clothes for all the children to meet our budget. We had to resort to buying a large freezer, so we could buy food in large quantities and freeze it. We could no longer go fishing or out doors for recreation without enlisting the help of our friends. The family car was now too small. We could not afford a large vehicle to accommodate the extended family.

Despite all our efforts to take care of my father's children they did not seem to appreciate the difficulties that we were facing. They developed a tendency to go outside the home and complain to whoever cared to listen to them, suggesting that they were not treated equally or justly. Those that received the complaints never bothered to check if the complaints were fair or justified – except for my aunt Winnie.

Such incidents brought a great deal of stress and distress to Veronica who was already feeling the strain of looking after an extended family. Without any doubt, this caused a great strain in our marriage. I could not believe what was happening. Why were these children doing this, I thought and what can I do about it? I began to regret my decision to take them in but it was too late to do anything about it except pray to cope with the situation at hand. It was not until 2007 when I worked for the Department of Children's Services in Surrey County Council in the UK that I began to understand the challenges faced by foster parents worldwide. We were woefully unequipped to undertake such a daunting task but, in hindsight, what else could we have done? The children resented carrying out household chores allotted to them. The girls left home as soon as they became of age. The boy remained at home until he found a girl to marry. Nevertheless, we did our best to look after them.

Because they did not work hard and excel at school they found it difficult to find jobs, I recruited them all, except for the eldest, whom I had found a job whilst my father was still alive, and trained them to work in my accounting practice. Through the training that I gave to them, they were able to leave and find reasonable jobs elsewhere. The boy was able to leave my practice and find a job as a Bookkeeper in Harare and was eventually able to migrate to Canada.

Despite all the sacrifices we made for these children, none of them have shown any gratitude.

CHAPTER 17

My Business Ventures

FOLLOWING THE ADVENT of independence, I became rather obsessed with the idea of starting a business and working for myself. I no longer had the desire to remain in the Civil Service because it had become heavily politicized. I started to look around for opportunities to start a business of my own – to become self-employed.

In 1980 I met Dave Saddington, a white man, with whom I became very good friends. He came up with the idea of us going into a business of poultry farming. We invited a mutual friend into the partnership. His name was Johannes. Johannes had some experience in rearing chickens and we decided that he would be the manager. My role was to be that of accountant to take care of all financial matters. Dave, because he was white and almost all businesses at that time were still in the hands of white people, was to be responsible for marketing all our eggs, meat and other poultry products.

Dave worked for a company called Nedlaw and was high up on the corporate ladder. I was employed by the Ministry Defence in the Legal Department. Johannes was not in employment as he had retired. The arrangement was that, as manager, he would receive a stipulated monthly salary.

We purchased 10 acres of land in Ruwa, about 17 miles from Harare. There was a beautiful three bedroomed house on the property. This became the manager's house. We registered the business as a private limited company under the name of Monica Farm (Private) Ltd.

We constructed Free Range Chicken sheds on the property sufficiently large to house three thousand layers as well as a section for broilers. We also constructed an abattoir on the farm. We employed about three African Farm hands to assist Johannes. We negotiated a $5,000.00 overdraft facility. For all intents and purposes, we were set for business. We honestly believed that our future was set. I was very hopeful that we would succeed and that my struggles were over.

Johannes and I thought that Dave, being a white man with connections and knowledge of marketing, would be the one who would propel the business to success. For a start, he had overlooked the need for us to have adequate freezing facilities. Although production at the farm was going well, the marketing side was a great let down. It was because of this failure that we had eventually closed the business and sold the farm.

The chicken project was a great disappointment to me. However, I was not going to give up. I desired so much to be independent by working for myself. Working for ADA was not good enough because it was an organization having some political authority and serving the state indirectly.

One morning in 1982 I came across an advertisement offering a Babies' Wear boutique on 57 Speke Avenue in Harare. The shop was called Bambino Babywear. After responding to the advertisement Veronica and I were invited to the house of the Greek couple that owned the shop. After chatting to them the idea of purchasing the shop appealed to us. We accepted the offer and bought the shop. Veronica ran the shop as she had some experience as a Sales Assistant at the Farmers Co-op and other retail outlets where dresses were sold. Again, I took care of the financial aspect of the business. What we did not realise at the time was that the customers for this type of business were mostly white. At this time a lot of whites had left or were in the process of leaving the country in large numbers resulting in low sales. Reluctantly we had to sell the shop.

Soon after Independence, Coloureds were able to buy or build a house in any suburb. There were no longer any restrictions; so, we bought a lovely four bedroomed house in a lush suburb of Highlands. We moved into the house on 44 Ridgeway South, highlands, on 1 July 1984. By this time, I had been promoted to the post of Administration Controller/Company Secretary. Libra was the General Manager. He had two deputies, Martin, an Accountant by profession, and Joseph, an Agriculturalist. My position fell below these two, but I reported directly to the Chairman of the ADA Board.

Martin and I were very close. Sometime in June 1984, shortly before I moved into my new home in Highlands, he approached me with a proposal to acquire an accounting business which he had seen in an advertisement. The business belonged to an Englishman, who was fed-up with the politics of this country and was returning to England. His name was Paul Stewart Longstaff. The business was called P. S. Longstaff & Co.

The asking price for the business was $25,000.00. Paul had about 100 clients, most of whom were white farmers. He had no employees except for Doreen, his Secretary. Martin did not want our partnership to be disclosed for fear that the white clients would take away their businesses to other accountants. He believed that I had a better chance of holding on to the clients if I purchased the business as a sole trader.

I purchased the business as a sole trader. I paid Paul Longstaff a deposit of $8,000.00; the balance of $17,000.00 payable over six months. Part of the agreement was that Paul Longstaff would remain fronting the Business until the end of six months to allow for a smooth handover. During this takeover I would often pop-in to the office, which was situated in Francis House and next to Greatermans, to be introduced to the clients. I was still employed by the Agricultural Development Authority but would have to find or make time to attend to our business. The actual professional work for the business would be performed by both Martin and I during the evenings and at weekends, but I would pop into the office to discuss the client's financial statements whenever it would be convenient to the client. Doreen would arrange the appointments beforehand.

At last, I thought, here comes my sought after independence. I was very happy indeed because I thought that this venture was a winner.

Martin and I shared a secretary. She was well acquainted with our involvement in the running of our partnership business. Apart from her usual duties at ADA she would liaise with Doreen at PS Longstaff & Company. So, it was that, whilst I was meeting with business clients, my secretary at ADA would phone me if there was any urgent matter to attend to at ADA. Similarly, if I am at ADA and a business client wanted to meet with me, Doreen would pass the message to me, through my secretary at ADA. Both premises were within a five or ten-minute drive from each other.

In 1987 ADA was granted a loan to acquire vehicles and farm equipment for its expanding farming operations. After all the vehicles had been purchased and allocated, there remained a few vehicles which were surplus to requirement. I approached the General Manager and requested that I be permitted to buy one of the surplus vehicles, a Peugeot 404 station wagon, which would be ideal to use for holiday travel, as I now had an extended family. Martin was aware of my request as the matter had to be approved by the ADA Board of Directors before the purchase could take effect. I was not the only person that had been given approval to purchase a vehicle.

Dr. Jacklitsh, one of the departmental heads, had also been granted permission to purchase a vehicle from the Proceeds of the French Financial Protocol. In 1988 I was accused of misusing my position by purchasing the vehicle without authority and given an option to resign which I did. I handed in my company car and took a bus ride home. This was a very difficult and traumatic moment of my life.

I felt betrayed. Both Libra and Martin had behaved as though I had stolen the car. I went home that evening not knowing what I was going to do next. What would I tell Veronica? That I no longer had a regular job? How long would it take before I secured another job? Did I really need to get another job, I thought? Getting home, I broke the news to the family.

The following day I went to PS Longstaff & Co. I wrote and posted a letter to Martin offering to pay him out for his share in the business. He accepted my offer and I sent him a cheque which he soon deposited into his personal account.

Business was very slow at first. Judging by past performance when the business was being run on a part-time basis, I was not going to make enough income to cover my mortgage, Doreen's salary, office rent, utilities and household expenditure. There was nothing that I could do but pray for a miracle. The thought that I may not be able to raise the money to pay mortgage instalment for the month haunted me

Nothing much happened in the following weeks. However, just a few days before my house mortgage fell due, I had a surprise visit from one of Paul Longstaff's old clients, who I thought had taken his business away from me because I was Coloured, came in to the office bringing his books with a substantial cash deposit as a down payment for the work. His account was big and the work was likely to keep me busy for a month or two to come.

This meant that I was now able to meet all my financial commitments. In fact, I needed to start looking for an assistant which I did. The business had truly taken off and I was confident that I was on my way to success.

A few days later, I received a letter informing me of the charges that had been raised against me by ADA. The charges were that I had abused my position and fraudulently acquired the Peugeot 404 station wagon. This was not true, of course. As far as I could see this was a trumped-up charge and would not be able to stand up in a court of law. Immediately, I handed the letter to my legal practitioner, to handle my case.

I could not understand why Martin, who had been my friend and confidante, was party to this. It took a couple of years before my case came before a high court judge. When the case came before Justice Godfrey *Chidyausiku* he threw it out. I didn't even have to attend court. I had been vindicated. I was very happy to put this matter behind me.

Gradually more and more of the clients that had left during the transition period returned bringing much needed work. When I took over the business Paul was using the old Burroughs machines. He was of the "old school" and had relied mainly on using manual systems of accounting. As I acquired more clients I began to introduce computers into my business and purchased two Amstrad stand-alone machines. Later I replaced these with the x264 PCs which were more powerful.

By the early 90's I had introduced more powerful PCs and linked them using the Novell NetWare system. All my computers were networked. My business grew by leaps and bounds and by the mid- nineties I had more than 400 clients split between individuals, sole traders, partnerships and small to medium sized businesses. A large proportion of these were farmers.

By the time farm invasions began in 1998, I had a staff of 15 including an IT technician. As my business started to grow I started to think of ways of increasing my income and investing for my retirement.

I purchased two Mitsubishi Colt T120 vehicles from Japan. I used them as minibuses to ferry passengers between the city and the surrounding suburbs, for business. I employed two drivers and obtained the necessary registration and licences. Business was good, and I was able to purchase a flat as an investment and a house in the high density suburb of Mabvuku for my sister Kathleen to live in with her three children. I also purchased a Mercedes diesel sedan for myself and two other vehicles for my wife and daughters.

CHAPTER 18

Zimbabwe Political and Economic Decline

THERE WERE 33M hectares of arable farming land in Zimbabwe at the time of independence. Of this, 6,000 white commercial farmers owned 45%. This comprised 11m ha of the most prime land.

Of the land in the drier regions, 8,500 mainly small black commercial farmers controlled 5% of the land.

50% of the poorest and infertile land in the former reserves from the colonial era was occupied by 700,000 black families.

Soon after 1980, the government entered into the "willing buyer, willing seller" agreement and made a commitment to resettle 162,000 farmers by 1990. For a number of reasons, the government did not reach half its targets. These included failure to implement the "willing buyer, willing seller" agreement, corruption within government, lack of funds and capital to purchase the land and develop it as well as general bureaucracy.

Only $47 million dollars had been donated by Britain by 1990. This represented only 44% of what had been requested. $630 million had been pledged at independence and the IMF and World Bank suspended aid for reasons of corruption and went on to impose ESAP – the Economic Structural Adjustment Program. The program had strict budgetary guidelines for government but land reform was not included in it. At this time, agriculture was a booming foreign currency earner for Zimbabwe and the tobacco and the cotton cash crop exports, alongside beef and horticulture, constituted 15% of

GDP in 1990 and 40% of the foreign currency earned.

The Zimbabwe economy was growing; so was the agricultural return. Given that more than 50% of the land was in the hands of whites, the landless blacks did not benefit from these returns despite the fact that they had provided the labour. The farm workers made up 25% of the national formal force. This constituted 11 -18 % of the population of the 90's.

From 1991 to 1998 the government rolled out a new and revised land reform. It passed the Land Acquisition Act in 1992. This was supposed to accelerate the land reform process through Land Designation and Compulsory Acquisition. This Act enabled government to acquire, for compensation, land that it deemed unproductive. Earlier studies conducted by the World Bank had shown that large scale farmers were using less than half the land they owned.

The following land was designated for compulsory acquisition:

-Derelict land or under-utilized land.
- Land owned by farmers with more than one farm.
- Land contiguous to communal lands.

The law only applied to rural land. For almost similar reasons as in the 1980's not much progress was made in terms of thrusting forward the resettlement of landless families. Only 71,000 families, out of the targeted number of 162,000 were resettled. Out of the total Zimbabwean population of approximately 12 million in 1997, 4,000 white farmers still owned over half of the land averaging 2,000 ha each. 1 million black families in communal lands were still living in overcrowded conditions with each family occupying on average 3 ha. This phase of the reform had failed too.

Britain, the US and other donor countries deemed the land reform corrupt and unfair if the government compulsorily acquired farms. They stopped donating to the land reform. Prime Minister Tony Blair terminated the funds available from Margaret Thatcher's administration when they were exhausted. He repudiated all commitment to land reform.

The repudiation by the British government led to the Zimbabwe government, which was now facing economic problems due to the ESAP program, to run out of money for land reform. This also resulted in the resettled families not getting much assistance from the government in terms of loans, training and infrastructure.

I believe that it was at this point in Zimbabwe's history that Mr Mugabe, realizing that the sponsored land reform had stalled and come to an end and his ZANU-PF party was rapidly losing popularity to the opposition party, the Movement for Democratic Change (MDC) led by Morgan Tsvangirai that he decided to forcibly grab the land. The strategy he chose to employ was to unleash his war veterans who were tasked with murdering the white farmers to get them off the land. The white farmers, were naïve enough by openly supporting the MDC; a move that was widely publicized by the media. I remember saying to people around me at that time that this would bring turbulent times for Zimbabwe although many did not believe my prediction and simply brushed it aside.

After I left my job at the Agricultural Development Authority (ADA) I went into Private Practice as an Accountant. In order to keep physically fit and focused a few of my friends and I decided to regularly play squash during our lunch break. We figured that playing squash would give us maximum fitness in the shortest possible period. After each session I would go and pick up my youngest daughter, Genevieve, from school, at the Seventh Day Adventist School in Highlands, and take her home and then return to work.

Sometime in May 1991, Dominic, Gilbert and I went to the squash court at Lytton Road in the industrial sites in Harare. As was usually the case we would play squash on a rotational basis.

I'd had a game with each of my mates. As I was playing a second game with Dominic, I slipped and banged my head against the wall and began to lose consciousness. An ambulance was called. In my delirium I was mumbling about picking up my daughter from school. Dominic left to pick up my daughter and Gilbert or "Gillie" as we affectionately addressed him, who was a Registered Nurse, remained to render first aid pending the arrival of paramedics. On arrival at Avenues Clinic I was taken into the emergency rooms where I was attended to by two physicians. As I was falling into deep unconsciousness I overheard one of the doctors saying to the other, "He is pretty bad; if he makes it he will most likely become a cabbage". At that point I became unconscious and only recovered consciousness after three days.

This is what Genevieve stated about this, "I was surprised Mr. Galloway came to pick me up that day. I remember he looked worried but each time I asked him where you were he kept saying you were in a meeting." Later in her Facebook post to Gilbert, she wrote, "I remember how you saved his life. You kept him awake until the paramedics got there. He is very blessed to call you a friend."

Dr. Auchterlonie was my attending physician. He told me part of his treatment regime was to stop me from vomiting as vomiting would release the pressure from my temple causing irreparable damage to my brain. I was hospitalized for two and half weeks instead of six months as the doctor had predicted on my admission. However, I spent a month at home recuperating. The outcome from my accident has been the loss of my sense of smell and the production of excessive wax from my right ear; thus causing deafness to my right ear.

In September 1996 I had enrolled my youngest daughter, Genevieve, at Oakwood College, Huntsville, Alabama in the United States. She was pursuing a three-year degree course in bio-chemistry.

In March 1997 my eldest daughter wanted to leave the country and find work in London. My sister, Ava, and her husband Victor, had immigrated to the UK. Ava was in England through her marriage to Vic. However, my eldest daughter needed a visa to work in the UK and she thought that if she could prove her British ancestry she would be able to secure a visa that would enable her to enter the UK and find work. To prove her ancestry, she decided to visit the National Archives in Harare to examine their records. At that time, we went under the family name "Hall". We did not know my grandfather's full names. All we knew was that my aunts and my grandmother had often referred to him as "Pat" or "Bert" or "Hall". There was another crucial piece of information that had been passed down to me by my father; the circumstances surrounding his death. It was a well-known fact that he had died in a gun accident whilst checking his gun traps one evening in September 1928. Also, my father had thought that René was his half-brother. As Native Commissioner, René was in charge of resettling, amongst others, African people from Filabusi to Jotsholo. Most of the black people in Filabusi believed René to be the son of *uMsoli* or *umaMkwananzi*. Often, they would approach my father bemoaning the fact that his 'brother' was the cause of their trouble.

Armed with this information my daughter searched the records and brought back information which convinced me that we had established our ancestry and that my grandfather's name was Harry Patrick Holl. I then decided to find out if my grandfather had any surviving children or relatives, especially in Harare or Bulawayo. I searched the Harare Telephone Directory. I came across the name "Patrick Harry Holl". I was more than convinced that he was Patrick Holl's grandson. He lived in a house in the neighbouring suburb of Greendale; not far from where I lived.

The question in my mind was how I should approach him? A direct approach would not work knowing how bigoted most whites were against black or coloured people. I had a very close friend by the name of Gordon. Gordon had had some dealings with Patrick Harry Holl and they knew each other pretty well. After discussing my problem with him he suggested that I write a letter to Patrick Harry Holl and he, Gordon, would deliver it. As agreed I wrote the letter and Gordon delivered it in person. Gordon later told me that Patrick had accepted the letter without question but did not open the envelope in his presence. Months went by, but I did not hear anything from Patrick. As far as I was concerned that was the end of the matter.

In October 1997 Veronica and I decided to visit Genevieve in the USA to see how she was getting on. Whilst in Huntsville we did some shopping and we were shocked to discover that the Zimbabwean dollar had fallen from two to one to six to one on the exchange rate. On our return to Zimbabwe the following month we found that the political landscape had changed. There was unrest. One day when my other daughter, Helen, who was working for me at the time, and I, where leaving the office to walk to the Parkade to pick up the car and go home we were besieged by rioters and police throwing tear gas. After some struggles as we tried to get away to safety we eventually made it home in Highlands.

After the first farm invasions I noticed a decline in business as we began to lose a few farming clients. Our Debtors register was also going up with most of our clients no longer paying on time. Also, the value of the Zimbabwean dollar was steadily declining to the extent that I was beginning to feel the strain in meeting my payments to Oakwood College for Genevieve's fees.

In May 1998 I decided to change my name by notarial deed and I assumed the surname of "Holl" by which I became known. Genevieve, who was not married at that time, also changed her name by deed poll. The other two girls, who were already married by now, did not consider it necessary to change their names. As all my children were over the age of eighteen, there was no benefit to them as regards obtaining a visa to live in the UK. My children were affected, as I was affected, by the rapidly deteriorating economic and political environment. They were also making frantic efforts to get out of the country using whatever means at their disposal.

I approached Shireen Ahmed and Associates, legal Practitioners to apply, on my behalf, for an Ancestry visa to enter the UK. The main reason for doing so was that my business was shrinking due to the political environment. The remaining clients were no longer paying for my services on time. This resulted in a severe cash flow making it very difficult to pay salaries and wages and other liabilities such as rent, utilities and my mortgage.

I was no longer able to pay Oakwood College because the value of the Zimbabwe dollar was shrinking against the US dollar. Genevieve was half-way to completing her degree in bio-chemistry but I was unable to keep up with my payments. My only option was to find work in a country where I could earn hard currency to pay fees for Genevieve. Due to my age it was no longer a feasible option for me to find employment outside the country and in a country that would pay me in hard currency. There was a real risk that Genevieve would be returned to Zimbabwe without completing her studies. It was primarily for this reason that I wanted to go and work in the UK.

Although I had now found my roots I needed to get two people to sign affidavits to support my application for an Ancestry Visa to enter the UK. There was no one that I could approach to do this for me. Although I knew that there had to be elderly white relatives, such as my father's half brothers or sisters still living, I had no way of contacting them. My efforts to contact them through the only person, Patrick Harry Holl, whom I had discovered from searching the telephone directory, had not responded to my letter that I had sent to him. There were times that I was tempted to go to his house, but I would, invariably, desist from doing so to avoid confrontation. I eventually decided to leave things as they were and forgot about applying for an Ancestry visa for the time being.

In December 1998 I had an unexpected visit from Phyllis Patricia Lewis and her sister Mona Frances Taylor. They came to see me at my PS Longstaff & Company offices at Pollack House in Robson Manyika Avenue. Patrick Harry Holl had visited his aunts in South Africa and, whilst there, he handed my letter to him to them. They had discussed the contents of my letter between the three surviving sisters and had decided that the two sisters, who lived in Harare, should pay me a visit; possibly to verify the authenticity of my claim. I was able to convince them that my claims were genuine. I suspect that they had known all along about the existence of my father and his three siblings.

At the end of the meeting Phyllis hugged me and said, with tears in her eyes, "You are, indeed, my nephew". This was a very emotional moment for the three of us. Before they departed they told me that they would be in touch with me as soon as they had made appointment for me to meet with René at Phyllis' house in Avondale. I surmised that the two sisters needed to confirm with René before formally acknowledging me as a genuine relation.

I shall always be grateful to Patrick Harry Holl for taking my letter to his aunts in South Africa. Although he never publicly acknowledged me as a relative, for reasons best known to him, he does know that we are blood related and nothing can change that.

A week later I received a call from Phyllis asking me to come to her house in Avondale. On arrival I was seated in the lounge and in front of René, Phyllis and Mona. René had many questions directed at me which I answered honestly and to his satisfaction. It was obvious to me that Rene knew a lot more about my father and his siblings than he cared to reveal. This was evidenced by the fact that he related an incident in which documents, concerning the four siblings, were deliberately burnt in a hut. It would seem that, at the time, Harry Patrick Holl may have been in the process of setting up a Guardians Fund for His Coloured children when someone, who was totally opposed to this, set the house on fire.

After our meeting, on 18 December 1998, I got Phyllis Patricia Lewis to sign an affidavit to support my application for an ancestry visa to live in the UK. I still required another affidavit but this had to be from a person who was not a relative. This meant that I would still not be able to submit my application and time was now running out. Nevertheless, I still got Phyllis to sign one just in case I come across someone who had known Harry Patrick Holl.

I believe in providence. I believe that when we pray with complete trust in God prayers are answered in ways that we sometimes cannot comprehend. I do believe that what happened to me in this instance was nothing short of a miracle.

One day in August 1999 I went to Bulawayo on a business trip. On my return I happened to be seated next to a Mr Hove. When I introduced myself to him he responded by telling me that he had knowledge of my grandfather who had been a well-known farmer in the *Esigodini* area which was then known as "Essexvale". Intrigued by this revelation I prodded him further and asked him if he was willing to sign an affidavit supporting my claim that I was Harry Patrick Holl's grandson. Realizing that, perhaps, he was not qualified to sign such an affidavit; he said that he didn't think that he would be the right person to sign my affidavit as he had not been closely associated with Harry Patrick Holl in his life time. He, however, knew of someone who was. Before landing at Harare Airport we made arrangements for both of us to go down to visit Chief Khayisa Ndiweni at *Ntabazinduna*.

On 27 September 1999 I picked up Mr Hove and drove to Ntabazinduna to meet with Chief Khayisa Ndiweni. Chief Ndiweni was not able to provide me with an affidavit either as he, also, did not know Harry Patrick Holl but knew of him. He however told us to go and see a Mrs. Stella Mary Coulson at her son's farm at Esigodini. He was certain that Mrs. Coulson would know Harry Patrick Holl as she was living in the area at the time when he farmed at Springvale Farm.

We drove to Esigodini to meet with Mrs. Coulson. Mrs. Coulson was a white woman in her nineties. She was very fluent in the isiNdebele language and she was impressed with my command of the isiNdebele language. When Mr Hove explained the purpose of our visit she immediately revealed the extent of her intimate knowledge of Harry Patrick Holl and his family. She knew of my father and his three sisters and that was enough for me to ask her to sign my affidavit. I drove her and Mr Hove to the District Commissioner's office where she signed the affidavit after which I drove her to her home and returned to Harare with Mr. Hove.

After securing the two affidavits, one from Phyllis Patricia Lewis and the other from Stella Mary Coulson, I handed them to Shireen Ahmed and Associates to submit my application via the British High Commission in Harare. Ava was, at this time, living in London not far from the immigration court in Feltham, Middlesex, in London.

After our acquaintance Phyllis visited me and my family on several occasions at our home at 44 Ridgeway South, Highlands in Harare. We had an opportunity to meet her daughter, Diana, and her son-in-law Paul and their 2 children- Daniel and Alex, Diana's brother Andrew. We also met Ida Bragge's daughter when we went to visit Diana and Paul at their home. Diana and Paul left Zimbabwe and migrated to Holland after which we lost contact. Andrew came to the UK, but we never met again.

It was not long after I submitted my application that I was granted a stay in the United Kingdom for which I am still a citizen. I started to prepare for my departure and I wanted to leave my clients in the hands of a competent accountant. By this time Martin had retired from the Agricultural Development Authority and wanted to re-join PS Longstaff & Co as a partner. We were, once again, good friends and I had forgiven him for his past behaviour and admitted him to the partnership at an agreed fee which would be deducted from his share of profits from the business over a period of twenty-four months.

My plan was that Helen and her husband, Jason, would be entrusted with looking after the house at 44 Ridgeway South, Highlands, in Harare. The house would be left intact with all its furniture and my car. Helen was to continue with her employment at PS Longstaff & Co which would be under the control of Martin. The business would pay, monthly; the amount owed by Mr. Matanda for the purchase of his share of the business as well any income that would accrue to me, into my bank account with the Standard Chartered Bank. I gave Helen a Power of Attorney to handle all my affairs. The amount that would accrue to me and deposited into my bank account would be used to defray all expenses such as the mortgage repayments, Old Mutual Retirement Pension Scheme and house rates, etc.

My wife and I had planned to take whatever job we could find in the UK, pay Genevieve's college fees at Oakwood and return to Zimbabwe within a period of two years. In May 2000 I booked and took a flight to London. The air fares had gone up tremendously to about Z$30, 000 each in a matter of a few weeks. Veronica followed me in August of that year.

I arrived in London and was met by my sister, Ava, and went to live with her and her husband, Victor, who was, by this time, ill with emphysema. Vic had been a heavy smoker for as long as I had known him even when he was a coach for Arcadia United Football Club.

They lived in a house on Linkfield Road, Isleworth, in Middlesex. I started to look for a job within my field. However, the process was long, and I could only secure a few interviews. I have often thought that this was because I was now 54 years old and had been self-employed for the last twelve years and did not have a current reference from a third party employer to vouch for my experience. Exasperated, I decided to accept employment as Security Officer working in a shopping mall complex. A month later, Veronica joined me and immediately found work at Charlotte House, a care home for elderly people with dementia.

At the beginning of November 2000 Veronica and I moved into a flat at 1B Bristow Road, Hounslow in Middlesex. With both of us working we were able to pay Oakwood College to cover Genevieve's fees and other financial requirements. Whilst paying the school fees we received word from Oakwood College that an anonymous donor had paid-off the school fee debt that was outstanding and that Genevieve would graduate without us no longer required to make any further payments. Again, this was providential.

In May 2001 we went to Oakwood College for Genevieve's graduation. Whilst in the USA we decided to visit some friends in Los Angeles. Although this should have been an enjoyable break we were somewhat subdued because of what was happening in Zimbabwe. Nonetheless we had good times visiting places like Disneyland and other places of interest.

In November 2002 we moved into a house on 54 Hampton Lane, Hanworth in Middlesex. By this time, I had found a job, as an Accountant, with SmithPointer & Co. This was a small accounting firm like the one that I had run in Zimbabwe. Veronica and I were working to raise enough money to return to Zimbabwe. However, the news we were receiving from Zimbabwe was that the economic situation back home was getting worse as the inflation rate had now reached 598.75%.

Following the introduction of the Fast Track Resettlement Program which began in 2000, the government had given 2,900 white farmers 90 days' notice to cease production and vacate their farms. Commercial Farmers Union membership dropped from 4,500 in 2000 to 3,200 in 2002. As a consequence, my business in Zimbabwe began to crumble.

Martin was forced to close the business offices and operate from his residence in Glen Lorne retaining a handful of clients. Helen found another job. Because I was no longer receiving any income from the business to maintain my house in Highlands, Helen had to sell all the furniture, cars and personal clothing and lease the house. She leased the house to a Coloured man by the name Melvin who was a member of the ruling party; very much to my disappointment. I don't think Helen realised the implications of leasing the house to a member of the ruling party.

Because Jason, Helen's husband, was not working at the time, Ava agreed for her and her family to move into her house in Cranborne, at a nominal rental. Ava's house was mortgage free; so, it was not difficult for her to do her niece a favour in the light of the difficult economic situation in the country. Helen had two children, Leah and Daniel, and the third one, Michael, was on the way. At this point it was obvious that all hopes of Veronica and I returning to Zimbabwe had been dashed by recent events.

I returned to Zimbabwe as soon as I could to finalize my affairs. Earlier on in my life I had taken out two Old Mutual Retirement Annuity Fund Contracts (Pension Scheme) with a combined value of Z$500,000 plus profits with a maturity date of 1 February 2011. When I approached Old Mutual to enquire about the state of my Retirement Annuity Contract, I was informed that the pension scheme had been suspended because of the stagflation. They offered to pay me out, and I really did not have any choices but to take the offer. The value of my pension had been drastically reduced by inflation and the total payout amounted to $278.00; which was not even enough to fill up my tank with petrol to travel to Bulawayo.

My intention was also to sell my house at 44 Ridgeway South. The housing market was at its lowest; besides what was I going to do with the valueless Zimbabwe dollar? This was before the country abandoned its currency in favour of the American currency, the US dollar. There was, however, one advantage arising from this bleak situation. The house mortgage value reduced considerably, in relation to the US dollar, making it easy to pay it off in Sterling or US dollars. I went over to CABS and paid off the mortgage and took possession of the title deeds.

The problem that faced me was that my tenant, Melvin, refused to pay the rent in US dollars claiming that it would be illegal to do so and that, since the lease agreement had stipulated payment in Zimbabwe dollars he was not prepared to pay his rent in US dollars. Melvin was politically connected to ruling political party. He had armed guards stationed at my house i.e. the house he was renting. Since I was not prepared to enter into a legal wrangle and risk losing my house to the party. Also the fact was that I was running out of time and, so, I left the matter unresolved and returned to the UK. However, I gave Melvin and his wife the first option to purchase the house in US dollars; which offer he failed to exercise. In any event Veronica was reluctant to sell the house as she still clung to the hope that we were going to return to Zimbabwe soon.

This is one example of how the lives of ordinary citizens of Zimbabwe were destroyed by the Mugabe regime. I can recall an incident relating to one Coloured man I knew that held a high position in the Salisbury Omnibus Company (later called Zimbabwe United Passenger Company or ZUPCO) who, like me, also lost his pension and lifesaving due to Zimbabwe's hyperinflation. He was much older than I was at the time and much closer to retirement age. For him to uproot and move to another country was unthinkable. Besides, it is most likely that he may not have had the option to leave Zimbabwe. Sadly, he decided to end it all by taking his own life.

CHAPTER 19

My Debilitating Illness

DURING THE MONTH of August 2004 I went to Little Park Surgery in Hampton on a routine visit to see my GP, Dr. Paska. I had been experiencing lower-back pains for some time. The previous week Dr. Paska had taken blood samples for lab analysis. The Doctor looked at me and then asked, "Have you ever taken drugs intravenously using hypodermic needles or syringes?" I replied, "No". "Why?" I asked. "The results of your blood analyses show that you have been infected by the Hepatitis C Virus" he replied.

I was shocked. He went on to say that he thought that I may have been carrying this virus for a long time – perhaps for more than 10 years. This could be the explanation for the back pain feeling that had dogged me since the early 90s. I had no idea of how I could have contracted the disease. Nonetheless this was a very disturbing revelation to me. I could only surmise that I may have contracted the virus during my army service when, as a soldier, I was regularly required to donate blood.

Prior to 1990, the HCV virus was commonly passed through blood transfusion. However, since 1990, all donated blood is tested for the Hepatitis C virus. It is extremely rare for it to be acquired through a blood transfusion.

"The virus will scar and destroy your liver and, in time, result in liver cirrhosis and, possibly, cancer of the liver", Dr. Paska said softly. "If your condition is not successfully treated soon you will probably require a liver transplant!" he concluded.

"How long do I have left?" I asked. "Probably ten to twelve years" he replied. I was devastated. How could this happen to me? I thought. "Why me Lord? I cried out as I left the surgery.

As I was going home I was thinking of how I should break the news to Veronica. How is she going to take it I thought?

I thought about Zimbabwe. Perhaps it would be better to return now, as we had originally planned, so that I could spend the last days of my life in the sunshine. On the other hand, I thought, it would be better to remain in England. Here, there were better medical facilities. At least I would die being cared for and my death would be less painful.

I had other things to think about. Going to Zimbabwe would mean certain death. Medical facilities were woefully inadequate. At least here in England there was a very good chance that I would be cured of the virus. In Zimbabwe I would not be able to pay for the treatment even if it was made available. Here in the UK I was covered by the National Health Service (NHS) and my treatment would be free.

I thought about my children and grandchildren. They were now scattered all over the globe due to Mr. Mugabe's ill-considered Land Reform Program. Some were in Australia and the others in the USA and South Africa.

Dr. Paska arranged an appointment for me to attend a biopsy at the Endoscopy Department at West Middlesex Hospital in Isleworth. After the biopsy it was arranged that I should attend a hepatitis C clinic at Chelsea & Westminster Hospital at 369 Fulham Road in London.

At about this time one of my daughters had given birth to her first child. I decided to postpone my Hepatitis treatment until after my visit to Australia. At least, I thought, I can die after seeing my granddaughter. So, Veronica and I flew to Sydney to see our granddaughter.

In August 2005 I began my treatment at Chelsea & Westminster. My treatment was supervised by Dr. Gardner, a hepatologist. He explained to me that I would be put on interferon (self-administered by daily injections subcutaneously on my thighs) and ribavirin (taken orally) medication, administered over a 48-week period. This treatment regimen is used to treat various cancers and virus infections including hepatitis C.

At the beginning of August 2006, which was the end of the 48 weeks, Dr. Gardner informed me that, because my hepatitis C was a genotype 1, my treatment had not been successful. I was put on a waiting list in the hope there would be a medical breakthrough in the treatment of this strain of Hepatitis C when I would be put on a new treatment regimen.

I suffered long term side effects from my interferon treatment. I was irritable and suffered mood swings and terrible hallucinations. I felt depressed and suicidal and often expressed a desire to die. I was unable to work and so I lost my job and stayed home all day. Because Veronica was the only one working at that time we struggled financially and our family commitments began to run up our credit cards; thus, placing ourselves in debt and difficulty.

Returning to our former home in Zimbabwe was no longer an option for the economy had totally collapsed with inflation running at a record level of 1,281.4% at the end of 2005. How could we possibly return to Zimbabwe now with my debilitating illness?

We had been told that my 48 weeks' interferon treatment, which was not successful, had cost the NHS about US$48,000. Besides, I was now on the waiting list for further treatment. I had to wait for the new treatment regimen although I had no idea for how long I would have to wait. Going back to Zimbabwe now would mean certain death as the country did not have a national health service.

My symptoms gradually improved to the extent that I was able to work. I got a job as a Finance Officer with the Surrey County Council in Chertsey. I started working for the Council from 1st July 2007. It was a good place to work and my employers were fully aware of my illness and were very understanding and cooperative. Whenever I needed time- off because of the illness I was given it.

It was no longer feasible for us to return to Zimbabwe because of my illness. In any event the political and economic situation was continuing to deteriorate. Zimbabwe had abandoned its own currency on April 12, 2009, and officially adopted the American currency as its own as part of a desperate bid to stave off a cash crisis.

By this time Helen and her husband Jason and their children had migrated to Australia. We decided that it would be best for us to emigrate to Australia to be with our children and grandchildren. The problem, however, was that we did not have the approximately A$100,000.00 required for the parent visa which would enable us to settle in Australia as permanent residents.

We were made to understand that the parent visa fee was to cover our medical expenses and, after residing in Australia for ten years, we would be entitled to a pension. This was to cover the fact that we would not have worked long enough in Australia to be entitled to a pension in our own right. It must be remembered here that we had lost all our savings and investments because of Robert Mugabe's mismanagement of the economy of Zimbabwe. Because we entered the country on a parent visa we were entitled to Medicare which meant that I would not be required to pay for my HCV treatment.

As the possibility of returning to Zimbabwe seemed remote, we decided to sell our house in Harare. We sold it for US$150, 000.00 which was way below the market price. We had no choice as we desperately needed to emigrate. After the required medical examination, we submitted the application and paid the necessary fee. We were granted our visa on the 24th March 2010 and had to enter Australia by not later than 24th March 2011. I therefore retired from Surrey County Council and arrived in Sidney, Australia, on 11th December, 2010.

I discussed my intended move to Australia with Dr. Gardner. He told me that he thought this was a good idea as I would be able to continue to receive medication for Hepatitis C. He also told me that he considered Australia to be very advanced in the medical field. He confirmed that all my medical records would be sent to counterparts in Australia and my name would remain on the waiting list.

In Australia my wife and I found a two-bedroom house in Fairfield West suburb of Sydney. We lived near our daughter and her husband. They introduced us to their GP, Dr. Lai Leong. Dr. Leong, in turn, referred me to a liver specialist, Professor Meng C Ngu who became my specialist physician.

In 2012 after my consultation with Dr. Ngu, he put me, once again, on 48 weeks' interferon and ribavirin treatment. Ten weeks into my treatment one morning I was unable to rise from my bed and had to be carried into a car and taken to Concord Hospital where I was diagnosed as suffering from gallstones. My interferon and Ribavirin treatment was halted to allow for my surgery. I was admitted, and Dr. David Joseph performed a cholecystectomy and took a biopsy which revealed that I had fibrosis of the liver. I also had further complications resulting in pulmonary effusion and had to have 1 litre of fluid drained from my thoracic cavity on two separate occasions.

At the beginning of 2016 Dr. Ngu informed me that the Government had approved a new treatment regimen. The new regimen did not involve the use of interferon and ribavirin. It involved Lediposvir/Sofosbuvir medication sold under the trade name Harvoni among others. In May 2016 Dr. Ngu put me on a12 week Harvoni medication to treat my HCV genotype 1 virus. After the 12 weeks I went for a blood test after a prescribed period of time and after a medical check-up I was informed that my Hepatitis C had been effectively cured.

EPILOGUE

ON NOVEMBER 21, 2017 the news channels throughout the western world provided wall-to-wall video and audio coverage to flash the news of the resignation of Robert Gabriel Mugabe as President of the Republic of Zimbabwe.

As I watched our people celebrating, delirious with joy, I wondered if they will lose that fear, that tinge of hopelessness in their eyes that has been with them for far too long. The terrible tragedy is that Robert Mugabe has stripped our people of their dignity which even the colonial oppressor failed to do. Some 3.7 million of us have had to leave home to seek refuge, sanctuary, survival and hope elsewhere; all for the sake of Land Reform?

How many of us have had to abandon our businesses, our livelihood and all that we had or worked so hard to develop and build because those in power destroyed the economic infrastructure through greed and corruption?

This despotic rule has been characterized by violence and theft at a grand scale. A report published by the new Zimbabwe President revealed that over USD$8 million dollars has been externalized by the deposed president's cronies.

USD$237,452,276 represented funds externalized through non-repatriation of export proceeds. USD$124, 846, 957 represents funds externalized through payment of goods not received in Zimbabwe. The remaining amount of USD464, 204, 171 is in respect of funds externalized to foreign banks in cash or under spurious transactions.

The published list indicated that most of illicit funds were externalized to China with numerous Chinese retail and mining companies dominating the list.

As I sat watching the news cast, I was not moved to share in the euphoria as welcoming as the news was. My thoughts were steeped in memories, really sad memories. I thought of my cousin who was killed in the Gukurahundi massacre alongside the other Matabele people. I thought of how my wife and I lost everything we had worked so hard for.